MEN-AT-ARMS SERIES

EDITOR: MARTIN WINDROW

W0038252

Prussian Reserve, Militia & Irregular Troops 1806-15

Text by PETER HOFSCHRÖER

Colour plates by BRYAN FOSTEN

OSPREY PUBLISHING LONDON

Published in 1987 by
Osprey Publishing Ltd
12–14 Long Acre, London WC2E 9LP
© Copyright 1987 Osprey Publishing Ltd

British Library Cataloguing in Publication Data

Hofschröer, Peter
    Prussian reserve, militia & irregular troops
    1806–15.—(Men-at-arms series; 192).
    1. Prussia. *Armee*—History
    2. Napoleonic Wars, 1800–1814—Campaigns
    —Prussia (Germany).
    I. Title   II. Series
    355'.00943   UA718.P9

ISBN 0-85045-799-8

Filmset in Great Britain
Printed through Bookbuilders Ltd, Hong Kong

Artist's note

Readers may care to note that the original paintings from which the colour plates in this book were prepared are available for private sale. All reproduction copyright whatsoever is retained by the publisher. All enquiries should be addressed to:

    Bryan Fosten
    5 Ross Close
    Nyetimber
    Nr. Bognor Regis
    Sussex PO21 3JW

The publishers regret that they can enter into no correspondence upon this matter.

Author's note

To avoid much duplication, uniform details given in this text assume access to the author's previous titles in this series: MAA 149 *Prussian Light Infantry 1792–1815*; MAA 152 *Prussian Line Infantry 1792–1815*; MAA 162 and 172 *Prussian Cavalry of the Napoleonic Wars (1) 1792–1807* and *(2) 1807–15*. Fuller bibliographical notes will also be found in these titles.

Prussian Reserve, Militia & Irregulars 1806-1815

Introduction

A substantial part of the armed forces at the disposal of the Prussian Army during the Napoleonic Wars, and in particular during the campaigns of the Wars of Liberation, 1813–15, consisted of irregular, semi-regular and reserve formations. Most historians tend to see these formations as being born out of the necessity of the uprising of 1813; but it should be pointed out that plans for the formation of a militia had been laid before the cataclysm of 1806, and only the speed of the catastrophe which befell Brandenburg-Prussia prevented these plans being executed. Moreover, there was little new in the so-called 'Kruemper' system, supposedly invented by certain leading reformers to circumvent the restrictions placed on the size of the defeated Prussian Army by a victorious Napoleon. The use of irregular bodies of men to engage in guerrilla warfare behind enemy lines was a tradition in the Prussian Army; Frederick the Great had used such troops, various comparable units fought in the campaigns of 1806 and 1807, and further forces were raised to participate in the campaign of 1813. The use of so-called 'foreigners' in the Prussian Army has often been criticised; but even after the

Stragglers making their way back to their depots and assembly areas after the defeats of autumn 1806. It was from among such men that the various Freikorps would be raised.

3

post-Jena reforms the necessities of war forced the Prussians to think again, and, as always, the 'foreigners' proved to be reliable troops. The uprising of 1813 was an act of great daring by a king whom history has often described as being timid and weak. All available forces were mobilised, and all available equipment was utilised. The Prussian Army of the Wars of Liberation was very much a patchwork affair.

Reservists

The army of reservists built up in Prussia between 1807 and 1813 was known as the 'Kruemper'. It was formed by dismissing a number of trained men at regular intervals and replacing them with raw recruits, thereby passing a large number of men through the ranks. Contrary to popular myth, neither the word nor the idea were novel. The word 'Kruemper' itself, related to the English 'crimp', and was first used in the days of Frederick the Great, eventually becoming the term which described

those extra recruits taken on to cover unexpected losses. Moreover, as we shall see later, this system was introduced before the French enforced restrictions on the size of the Prussian Army, and was therefore initially not a clever scheme to get around these restrictions.

This system of training men and then putting them on furlough, building up a trained reserve, had its origins—as much else in the 'reformed' Prussian Army—in the days of Frederick the Great. The catalyst of such planning was the need for a larger army, but one that would not require any more expenditure of the limited resources of a poor agricultural economy like that of Brandenburg-Prussia. Before the Seven Years War, Frederick had built up a strong reserve in this way; but after such a strenuous war the extra manpower was needed on the land, so the idea was dropped for the time being.

From 1787 the idea was taken up again, and a

A raid on a French supply train in the mountains of Silesia. The officer with his arm in a sling is Count Goetzen, the guerrilla leader. His men come from a mixture of units; to his rear are a grenadier, a musketeer and a fusilier.

system of reservists developed in the years prior to Jena. Alongside such work went the planning of a militia for use in defending the fatherland and garrisoning the fortresses. It was planned to formalise this system; but as with so much else in the army at this time, lethargy ruled the day, and only when war loomed in 1805 did anyone take any action. As always, it was too little, too late. The basic idea was for each company to take on more men than it required every year, and then to put the same number on furlough, passing a greater part of the male population through the ranks and calling on them in time of war. Such a system clearly took years to become effective and, at this stage, time was not on Prussia's side.

After the defeat of the army in 1806, this idea was taken up again. On 31 July 1807, a few weeks after the conclusion of the Peace of Tilsit, Scharnhorst published a memorandum suggesting a way of training additional men without spending any more of the state's limited funds. He estimated that in three years, a trained reserve of 17,000 men could be built up if every company put 20 men a year on furlough and took on 20 replacement recruits for training. Scharnhorst's idea came from a Colonel von Below, who had operated a similar scheme in his regiment from 1805, this memorandum was published more than a year before the Convention of Paris which restricted the Prussian Army to 42,000 men.

The next myth commonly heard is that the 'Kruemper' battalions consisted entirely of men who had only had a short training, and that the battalions formed from them in spring 1813 were thus of less value than the Line battalions. The regulations governing the 'Kruemper' state time and again that it was the oldest men in the company who were to be put on furlough, their places being taken by 18-year-olds. The consequence was that only part of the men put on furlough would be fit for recall at a later date. A report dated 28 March 1810 stated that of the 22,380 men put on furlough, only 11,213 were fit for duty. The figure improved as time went on, however. In mid-1811, there were 25,261 men fit for active service and 5,250 fit for garrison duty; and at the end of the year the figures were 31,259 and 8,410 respectively. This expansion was achieved by increasing the number of men being replaced: war between France and Russia

Maj. von Schill meeting his untimely death in Stralsund on 31 May 1809. His death marked the end of an abortive attempt at an uprising in northern Germany. A colour reconstruction of his uniform is published in Men-at-Arms 172, Plate E2.

appeared likely, and the need for more men was apparent.

The first real attempt at subterfuge and circumvention of the restrictions imposed by the Treaty of Paris took place in 1811, when the so-called 'Training Depots' were formed. These units were to replace the regiments assigned to coastal protection and the enforcement of the 'Continental System', Napoleon's attempted blockade-in-reverse of Britain. Napoleon took a dim view of such activity, however, and the 'Training Depots' were disbanded—although not before their members had gained valuable military experience.

The final acceleration of the 'Kruemper' system occurred in 1812. The men being put on furlough were to have had at least one year's training—an indication that there were fewer men of longer experience available for furlough than before. Reports dated September and October 1812 indicate that the 'Kruemper' system had produced 33,337 men fit for active service and 3,087 fit for garrison duties. The number mobilised in spring 1813 could not have been significantly greater. The myth, repeated even today, that the 'Kruemper' system produced 150,000 recruits is thus quite unfounded. Certainly, the 'Kruemper' and men still in the Line formations were used as the cadre of the new formations raised in spring 1813, but the bulk of the members of these formations were raw recruits.

The acid test of the success of the 'Kruemper' system came with the mobilisation of spring 1813. The annihilation of the Grande Armée in Russia is well enough documented elsewhere to need no repetition here. Prussia had started furtive preparations for war in 1811. The hope was that the opportunity would arise to take up arms against the foreign oppressor; but news of these preparations reached Napoleon, and they were stopped. However, an auxiliary corps of 20,000 Prussians was included in the largest army ever assembled and marched off with it into Russia—fortunately managing to avoid the fate which overtook the main body of the army. The commander of this force of Prussians, Gen. Yorck (see the short biography in Men-at-Arms No. 149, *Prussian Light Infantry 1792–1815*) negotiated the neutrality of his contingent, and this led to an uprising in East Prussia which sparked off the Wars of Liberation and Prussia's declaration of war on France.

In fact, King Frederick William III of Prussia had anticipated the need for mobilisation, and had ordered Maj.Gen. von Buelow, the governor of Lithuania, East and West Prussia to mobilise his troops and, in view of the Russian advance, to withdraw them behind the Vistula. The Line formations were to be brought up to strength, and the 'Kruemper' called up, along with new recruits. Napoleon agreed to this, as he needed further troops and anticipated using these men to reinforce the Prussian Auxiliary Corps.

Once news of the Convention of Tauroggen— Yorck's treaty with the Russians—became public knowledge, Frederick William ordered the first increase in the strength of the army. Depot battalions of 801 men were to be formed for each of the 11 infantry regiments; these were to consist of two-thirds 'Kruemper' and one-third recruits. Meanwhile, Buelow had not been idle. He had

Training the 'Kruemper'. This plate by Knoetel is conjectural, but this must be how the 'Kruemper' were dressed initially, in a mixture of old and new uniforms.

'Kruemper' and recruits on the march to Breslau, Silesia, in spring 1813.

raised eight reserve battalions of 801 men on the basis of the Instruction of 20 December 1812, and in February 1813 formed a ninth. The 2nd, 3rd and 4th Battalions—their cadre being the depots of the 2nd, 3rd and 4th East Prussian Infantry Regiments and the remainder coming from the 'Kruemper'—consisted entirely of trained soldiers. On 12 January 1813 they were designated the Depot Battalions of the 2nd to 4th East Prussian Regiments. The remaining battalions consisted of half 'Kruemper' and half recruits. One of these battalions was designated the Depot Battalion of the 1st East Prussian Infantry Regiment (whose actual depot had been taken prisoner in Memel) and the rest as 1st to 5th East Prussian Militia Battalions, the latter being renamed Reserve Battalions on 1 February 1813.

Maj.Gen. von Borstell, commander of the Pomeranian Brigade, received his mobilisation orders in January 1813. Using 'Kruemper' and recruits, he brought his Line battalions up to field strength, and then formed eight battalions of militia. Each of the first six of these had a cadre of five officers, eight NCOs, 40 privates and one musician along with 93 'Kruemper'. They therefore consisted largely of recruits. The 7th and 8th Battalions took their cadres from the cavalry regiments of the brigade.

Yorck marched into Koenigsberg, the capital of East Prussia, on 8 January 1813, and immediately set about mobilising all the available manpower. Firstly, he called up all the 'Kruemper' and recruits whom Buelow, the local military commander, had left behind in his rush to get behind the protection of the Vistula; and founded a large training camp in Koenigsberg, from which seven reserve battalions were raised on 1 March. These were the 1st to 4th East Prussian Musketeer Reserve Battalions and the 1st to 3rd Lithuanian Fusilier Reserve Battalions.

On 1 February 1813 the king ordered a second increase in the strength of the army. Each of the ten Line battalions in Silesia was to give up five officers,

Departure of the militia and volunteers, autumn 1813. Note the well-equipped volunteer rifleman on the left; and the militia hornist on the right, displaying features which may be compared with plates in Men-at-Arms 149.

20 NCOs and 60 men to form the cadre of a reserve battalion of 801 men. The remaining manpower was to consist entirely of 'Kruemper'. Reserve battalions were thus formed for the Life, 1st East Prussian, West Prussian and Silesian Grenadier Battalions, the 2nd West Prussian and 2nd Silesian Regiments, and two each for the 1st West Prussian and 1st Silesian Regiments. A Guard Reserve Battalion was also formed. Borstell, military commander of Pomerania, was also ordered to undertake a similar expansion: he formed five reserve battalions, one each for the 2nd East Prussian and Pomeranian Grenadier Battalions, the 1st Battalion of the 1st Pomeranian Infantry Regiment and the 2nd and Fusilier Battalions of the Colberg Regiment. These reserve formations were used both in the field and for garrison duties in the campaign of spring 1813.

The armistice of the summer of 1813 allowed the Prussians the opportunity to reorganise their army and to consolidate their new formations. A number of reserve battalions were incorporated into the Line regiments, and a number of so-called 'Reserve Regiments' were formed. The Foot Guard Regiment, which had previously been No. 8 in the Line, was taken out of the Line, and Regiments 8–11 were re-numbered. Moreover, a 2nd Foot Guard Regiment was formed using a number of Line battalions, and reserve battalions were used to replace them. The 3rd Battalion of the Life Regiment replaced the Fusilier Battalion. The 3rd Battalion of the Colberg Regiment was absorbed into the regiment, and a new Brandenburg Infantry Regiment (No. 12) was formed from the first two reserve battalions of the Life Regiment and the 3rd Battalion of the 1st West Prussians. Furthermore, on 1 July 1813, 12 Reserve Infantry Regiments, each of three battalions, were formed (although the 1st, 3rd and 5th Regiments had a fourth battalion which was later absorbed by the others to make up for losses). The battalions were numbered 1, 2 and 3, unlike the Line Regiments which had a 1st, 2nd

and Fusilier (Light) Battalion. Thus the following Reserve Infantry Regiments were formed:

1st: from 3rd Bn., 1st East Prussians; 1st East Prussian Res.Bn.; 1st Lithuanian Fusilier Res.Bn.; 2nd East Prussian Res.Bn. (disbanded May 1815).

2nd: from 3rd Bn., 1st and 4th Bns., 1st Pomeranian Regt.

3rd: from 3rd Bn., 2nd East Prussians; 3rd East Prussian Res.Bn.; 2nd Lithuanian Fusilier Res.Bn.; 4th East Prussian Res.Bn. (in August 1813 the 1st Bn. of this regiment was disbanded and its place was taken by the 3rd East Prussian Res.Bn.; the 4th became the 2nd Bn. of the regiment.)

4th: from 3rd Bn., 1st and 2nd Res.Bns., 3rd East Prussian Regt.

5th: from 3rd Bn., 1st and 2nd Res.Bns., 4th East Prussians; 3rd Lithuanian Fusilier Res.Bn. (the latter was disbanded in December 1813).

6th: from 1st and 2nd Res.Bns., 1st West Prussians; 4th Res.Bn., 1st Silesians.

7th: from 3rd Bn., 1st and 2nd Res.Bns., 2nd West Prussians.

8th: from 2nd and 3rd Res.Bns., 1st Pomeranians;

Battle around the churchyard, Grossbeeren, August 1813. This picture by Richard Knoetel is particularly interesting because it shows all the various stages of loading and firing a musket, as well as a number of militiamen with various types of equipment.

3rd Res.Bn., Colberg Regt.

9th: from 1st, 2nd and 4th Res.Bns., Colberg Regt.

10th: from 3rd Bn., 1st and 2nd Res.Bns., 1st Silesians.

11th: from 3rd Bn., 1st and 2nd Res.Bns., 2nd Silesians.

12th: from 4th and 5th Res.Bns. of Life Regiment; 3rd Res.Bn., 3rd East Prussians.

These regiments were consolidated into the Line in March 1815, and became Regiments 13–24.

The seven remaining reserve battalions (3rd and 4th Res.Bns., 1st West Prussians; 3rd Res.Bn., 2nd West Prussians, Life and 1st Silesians; 3rd and 4th Res.Bns., 2nd Silesians) were used to replace the great losses of manpower sustained during the campaign of spring 1813. On 28 May 1813, the formation of 11 replacement battalions was ordered, and each regiment gave up eight officers,

Major von Luetzow, founder and leader of Luetzow's Freikorps.

24 NCOs and 80 privates as a cadre. These battalions, along with the garrison battalions, were to be used to provide replacements for the losses sustained by the field battalions.

Uniforms

The men of the reserve formations were supposed to wear the uniform of their parent regiment but with a number on their shoulder straps to differentiate them. What they actually wore was quite a different matter. Prussia's very limited resources were already stretched to equip the Line regiments: there was simply not the time and money available to clothe tens of thousands more men. A number of reserve formations were clothed in the provisional uniform, which consisted of grey caps and jackets. Others wore somewhat outlandish British-made uniforms diverted from the Peninsula. Much use was made of captured French material. Battalions within regiments varied, and the cadres often continued to wear the uniform of the parent regiment, so even within battalions there was great variety. Attempts were made to adopt proper

uniforms after the end of hostilities in 1814; but the return of Bonaparte to France and the Hundred Days Campaign prevented the completion of such plans, and some former reserve units went into battle at Waterloo and Ligny in their old uniforms.

To present as complete a picture as possible of the uniforms of every reserve formation from the sources currently available would take up more space than is feasible in this short work; the following extracts from various histories should give a rough outline of the appearance of a typical reserve regiment, underlining the impossibility of dogmatic generalisations in this area.

The **3rd Battalion, 1st East Prussian Infantry Regiment** wore the following uniform, according to its regimental history (*Geschichte des Infanterie-Regiments Herwarth von Bittenfeld [1. West-faelischen] Nr.13 im 19. Jahrhundert*, v.Blume, Berlin 1910):

Spring 1813: Grey cloth jackets with no distinctions; tight grey cloth trousers; black cloth knee-length gaiters; grey cloth caps with leather peaks, red band and red number 1; grey cloth greatcoats with red collars, white shoulder straps and yellow buttons. The equipment consisted of cartridge boxes on white belts, and calfskin or twill knapsacks, the former with white belts, the latter with grey straps. The 'Old' Prussian musket served as armament. The officers wore blue tunics with red collars, cuffs and tail turnbacks, and blue shoulder straps with silver braid according to rank; dark grey trousers with red piping and a row of flat yellow buttons along the outer seams; covered field caps; grey greatcoats; sashes; sabre or epée. Grey overcoats were also worn instead of the blue tunics.

July 1813: The above uniforms were replaced by clothing supplied by Britain. Felt shakos had leather lining, leather peaks and bands, oval brass shields bearing the English lion, and red and white woollen pompons. The blue tunics had low, red, open collars, narrow dark blue shoulder straps with white piping, and one row of yellow buttons stamped with the number '14'; both sides of the tunic had white lacing; the red cuffs had small yellow buttons, and a band of white lace; there were square, short and very broad white tails. Blue cloth and white linen trousers were worn over black half-gaiters. The uniform was completed by a leather neckstock; a blue cloth field cap which had flaps on both sides, and a black band; a white cloth jacket, worn under the tunic; and a grey cloth unmarked greatcoat with a cloak collar. Furthermore, the battalion was supplied with new cartridge boxes with white belts, yellow canvas knapsacks with white straps, and British muskets. The NCOs wore short swords on a shoulder belt, a red sash, white piping on the tunic collar, three white chevrons on the left arm, and red and white feather plumes on the shako. The musicians' tunics had a number of bands of white lace on the sleeves.

This battalion was joined by another three in

Luetzow's recruiting office at the Gasthof zum goldnen Zepter in Breslau.

summer 1813 to form the **1st Reserve Infantry Regiment**. These battalions wore the uniform of the 1st East Prussian Infantry Regiment, namely: blue tunics with high, open, tile-red collars; cuffs of the same colour with blue patches; white shoulder straps, red tail turnbacks, and yellow buttons; felt shakos, with a white band for privates and gold lace for NCOs; grey cloth caps with a red band; tight grey trousers, with black cloth knee-length gaiters; grey cloth greatcoats with red collars, white shoulder straps and yellow buttons; cartridge boxes

A volunteer Jaeger of Luetzow's Freikorps wearing the corps' black uniform with red piping and yellow buttons, the colours of the German flag.

with white belts (black for the Fusiliers); calfskin knapsacks with white or black straps. The Musketeer Battalions were armed with French weapons, captured by the Russians in 1812 and later transported to Koenigsberg; the Fusilier Battalion received 'Old' Prussian muskets (i.e. the 1780 pattern). The officers wore the same uniform as those of the 1st East Prussian Regiment.

The new uniform issued from *spring 1815* was as follows. The blue tunics had yellow collars, closed at the throat by hooks; yellow cuffs with blue patches; red tail turnbacks, and two rows of yellow buttons. Felt shakos had leather tops, a cockade, brass fittings and badge, white linen cords and a waxed cloth cover. The grey cap had a red band; grey cloth and white linen trousers were cut in the shape of a gaiter at the foot; grey cloth greatcoats had yellow collars, yellow shoulder straps and yellow buttons. Grey jackets were issued, as were ankle-length boots with grey twill gaiters. The British belts were exchanged for those of Prussian style. The armament remained as before. The uniforms of the officers were of the same colour and the shakos the same style as those of the privates; the tails of their tunics were somewhat longer than those of the men and of a more frock-like cut. They also wore grey overcoats. In 1814 epaulettes were introduced. The badge and shako cords were silver for officers; and off duty they wore a felt fore-and-aft bicorne with a black feather plume. The grey trousers had a double red stripe with a line of red piping in the middle. The officers of the Musketeer Battalions were armed with the epée, those of the Fusiliers carried the sabre.

Clearly, there was some considerable variation in the clothing worn by members of this regiment; and after the periodic changes it is quite possible that items of old kit were retained, or passed on to the depot troops, only to be seen again at the front when the depot supplied replacements.

The reserve formations were, on the whole, not quite as well trained or equipped as their comrades in the Line units, but any initial differences in performance were most probably overcome after a couple of weeks on campaign. By the autumn of 1813, the reserve infantry regiments were more or less the equals of the Line.

Freikorps and Foreign Units

It was also a tradition in the Brandenburg-Prussian Army to form bands of irregular troops to meet specific requirements that the regular army was unable to fulfill. Frederick the Great's Friekorps are well-known: they were raised to act as spies and scouts, and to harass the enemy behind his lines. They were later seen as a basis for the formation of regular light troops (see my *Prussian Light Infantry 1792–1815*, Men-at-Arms 149). Similar bodies were raised for the campaigns of 1806/7 and 1813–15. They were used for raiding behind enemy lines, harassing French lines of communication, freeing prisoners-of-war, sabotaging enemy installations, etc.

Amongst the Freikorps raised for the 1806/7 campaign were those formed by the following officers:

In Prussia:

Rittmeister von Moellendorff. In 1806 he was an adjutant of the ill-fated Prince Louis Ferdinand. From November 1806 he gathered together soldiers scattered from the army, and used them to collect conscripts in Pomerania and West Prussia and to send them over to the east of the Vistula. He also used them for gathering intelligence on enemy movements, and to protect the local population from enemy marauders. He was sent a detachment of six NCOs, one bugler and 24 troopers from the Hussar Regiment Duke Eugene of Wuerttemberg under Lt. Count Pinto. According to the roll-call of 11 November 1806, he had a total of 106 men from various cavalry regiments and a detachment from the Infantry Regiment Kalkreuth. At the end of the month, he was ordered to send his infantry and his heavy cavalry horses to Koenigsberg, and to form a mobile 'Partisan Corps' which, from January to April 1807, formed part of Major von Borstell's Detachment. The latter had 190 Gardes du Corps and 70 Cossacks, who covered Koenigsberg. After Borstell returned to Koenigsberg in April 1807, Moellendorff was deployed on the Frische Nehrung. His squadron and that of Pinto consisted largely of Life Carabineers, Holtzendorff, Cuir-

Theodor Koerner, poet and dramatist, who met his death whilst serving in Luetzow's Freikorps.

assiers, Irwing and Hertzberg Dragoons, and Usedom and Rudorff Hussars. The Corps was disbanded at the end of July 1807 and its men were transferred to new cavalry formations.

Stabsrittmeister von Raven. An officer of the Garde du Corps, he brought together around 200 cavalry troopers from various regiments. He led them back to Koenigsberg, where he was given permission to form a Freikorps along with Rittmeister von Alvensleben of the Holtzendorff Cuirassiers. They brought together a detachment of 162 sabres mainly from the Silesian regiments, including Holtzendorff and Heising Cuirassiers, Prittwitz and Krafft Dragoons, Wuerttemberg, Gettkandt, Pletz and Bila Hussars. From January to April 1807 it was reinforced by 68 Gardes du Corps and placed under the commander of Major von Borstell. Subsequently it was joined by a second squadron under Stabsrittmeister von Ledebur of the Reitzenstein Cuirassiers, consisting of members of the Bailliodz Cuirassiers, Irwing Dragoons, Wuert-

Luetzow's Freikorps attacking a French supply train at Gadebusch on 26 August 1813. It was in this action that Koerner (shown here on the white horse) was killed.

temberg, Koehler, Usedom and Bila Hussars. This Freikorps was disbanded at the end of July 1807, its men being transferred to the provisional cavalry brigades.

Kapitain von Wilamowitz. An officer from Infantry Regiment Natzmer (No. 54), he was given permission on 10 November 1806 to raise a corps from local sharpshooters in New East Prussia. As the areas in which these men lived soon came under enemy control, Wilamowitz had to give up his plans. He was transferred to Danzig where he was provisionally appointed commander of the Krockow Freikorps.

Rittmeister Count von Krockow. This retired hussar officer was given permission to form a corps from volunteers in Pomerania. Recruiting began on 10 January 1807: by the 17th of that month Krockow already had a squadron of cavalry and a battalion of 300 infantry. This 'Frei-Jaegerkorps' was allowed a theoretical strength of five foot companies (21 officers, 50 NCOs, 11 buglers, ten sappers, 750 men,

four surgeons and three staff: total, 849 men) and one squadron of cavalry (six officers, one sergeant-major, 12 NCOs, 12 riflemen, 160 troopers, three tumpeters, one surgeon, one farrier: total, 196 men). The corps was also supplied with two 3 pdr. cannon and a mounted crew from the artillery depot in Danzig. The first rank of the infantry were armed with muskets, the others with rifles. The uniform consisted of dark green coatees with black collars, shoulder-straps and cuffs, and yellow buttons. The mounted Jaegers had yellow shoulder cords, grey overalls, and iron helmets with a death's-head badge painted on the front and a black horse hair plume.

The men were mainly freed prisoners-of-war from the Brandenburg and Pomeranian regiments. About 100 of the infantry were from the Prince of Orange's Regiment, others were from regiments such as Braunschweig-Oels, Pirch, Puttkammer, etc. On 26 March 1807 Count Krockow was wounded and taken prisoner; Col. Schuler von Senden took over provisionally, then Maj. von Mutius of Dragoon Regiment Rouquette; and from 31 May, Maj. von Wilamowitz. The corps was

Koerner and his comrades singing his latest 'hit' around the camp fire. (Unfortunately the copy of the picture used here has been damaged by a fold.)

disbanded on 1 August at Schmelz on the River Memel. The men from the Brandenburg and Pomeranian regiments (240 and 87 sick) were sent to the 2nd Neumark Reserve Battalion; some were transferred to the Guard, and the troopers to various cavalry regiments. On 24 August, in recognition of his services, Count Krockow was given permission to continue wearing the unique uniform of his corps.

Rittmeister von der Marwitz. In 1806 Marwitz had been adjutant to Prince Hohenlohe, and in March 1807 he asked the king for permission to raise a Freikorps. His request was granted, and recruiting began in East Prussia on 2 April. Marwitz was given 50 cavalry troopers for his cadre (37 Bila Hussars, 18 Rudorff and Bluecher Hussars and Hertzberg Dragoons) from the cavalry depots. Later he received a further 55 Rudorff hussars and five cuirassiers, and 150 dismounted men from the Hertzberg Dragoon Regiment. The cavalry was divided into five squadrons, one of which consisted of 44 Rudorff Hussars under Stabsrittmeister von Sohr from the 3rd Sqn. of the 1st Hussar Brigade (Col. von Corvin-Wiersbitzki), together with men

of this regiment who had found their way to the Freikorps; on 7 May, however, the king ordered that they should return to their regiment, as they still wore its uniform. At first, the infantry consisted of 33 men under Stabskapitain von Zglinitzky[1] of the Regiment Winning. On 18 May the Freikorps received permission to raise 2,000 cavalry (dragoons) in ten squadrons and 600 infantry (sharpshooters) in four companies. At the end of May the corps was sent to Swedish Pomerania where, on 8 June, Lt.Gen. Bluecher reorganised the corps, permitting it to consist of four squadrons of cavalry (eight officers, 20 NCOs, five drummers, 260 troopers). 1st Lt. von Schmeling, who had been sent on in advance to raise recruits and gather horses and supplies, managed to raise another squadron of Rudorff Hussars as well; this squadron was passed to 1st Lt. von Colomb. However, this squadron too was taken away from the corps, along with its

---

[1]Note that contemporary spellings are used in this text, e.g. Kapitain.

15

Bluecher Hussars (36) and Queen's Dragoons (43). Schmeling was then given the task of forming a squadron of Uhlans.

According to Bluecher's report of 28 July, the corps was at the following strength: Cavalry—four squadrons with a total of 15 officers, 45 NCOs, eight trumpeters, four farriers, four surgeons, 357 troopers, 433 horses. Infantry—two companies of Schuetzen with a total of ten officers, 16 NCOs, eight musicians, 131 privates. Depot—one officer, four NCOs, 29 privates.

The uniform consisted of long Litewka coats with yellow hussar braiding, and shakos with white plumes for the cavalry and green for the infantry. The infantry were armed with smoothbore muskets, the cavalry with hussar sabres, one squadron had lances. The corps was disbanded on 20 September, and Bluecher had formed from it a squadron of Bosniaks under 1st Lt. von Schmeling for the Rudorff Hussar Regiment. The Hertzberg Dragoons and other men of the East and West Prussian regiments were formed into two squadrons. The infantry were added to Grenadier Battalion

Members of Luetzow's Freikorps being blessed before going to war.

Wangenheim as its 5th Company. The king, however, did not agree to this reorganisation, and ordered the disbandment of the corps. Schmeling's squadron was instead split up between the other two squadrons of the Regiment Rudorff in Pomerania; Zglinitzky's Company was absorbed by the Wangenheim Grenadiers; and the Hertzberg Dragoons disbanded and the veterans sent home. *Kapitain von Meyern.* An officer of 6th West Prussian Reserve Battalion, formerly of Regiment Natzmer, who received permission in March 1807 to form a corps from huntsmen, gamekeepers, etc. The corps was to be based in Lyck and was to consist of 300–400 men. Recruiting was slow, as the Field Jaeger Regiment took the best recruits. On 20 April Meyern was ordered to send 100 of his men to Bluecher's Corps in Pomerania. A detachment of three NCOs and 50 men under Lt. von Beyer was sent to Pillau, a port on the Baltic coast and, when in Pomerania, were placed under the command of Kapitain von Valentini II. According to Meyer's report dated 12 May, he still had two officers, ten NCOs, two buglers and 53 men. By the time Lyck was evacuated on 20 June because of the proximity of the French, his corps had increased to 106 men. Their uniform was similar to that of the Field Jaeger

Regiment (see Men-at-Arms 149), but the coats were of the new cut, and they wore shakos and grey trousers. The corps was disbanded in Tilsit at the end of August. The professional gamekeepers were transferred to the Field Jaeger Corps, the remainder of the men were sent home.

Gen. Count Kalckreuth: On 3 April 1807 this officer, the Governor of Danzig, was given permission to form a Freikorps from freed prisoners-of-war who had not been allocated to any other duties. On 12 April he had 90 men at his disposal, under Lt. von Peirille of Regiment Diericke. They were clothed in the uniform of Regiment Treskow, and also wore long trousers and shakos. On 25 May this corps consisted of 41 NCOs and 157 privates. On 21 May the cavalry detachment consisted of three officers, nine NCOs, one trumpeter, 69 privates and seven horses. This corps was disbanded at the end of September and its men were sent to the 2nd Neumark and Silesian Reserve Battalions.

Von Schill's Freikorps

By far the most famous of the Freikorps of the 1806/7 campaigns was that formed by Maj. von Schill. An officer in the Queen's Dragoons, he had already started to form a Freikorps in the Colberg Area with freed prisoners from his regiment and the Bluecher Hussars when, on 13 January 1807, his enthusiasm was given official blessing. By 17 January he already had two squadrons ready for action and a third was being formed, but lacked any equipment. Moreover, he had managed to get hold of eight cannon; and Johann Ehrenfried Otto, a forester from Stepenitz, had started to organise a Jaeger company for him. By 7 February Schill's cavalry consisted of six officers, 30 NCOs, 388 troopers and 298 horses. His infantry consisted of four officers, 24 NCOs, 20 Schuetzen and 220 privates, as well as 55 Jaegers; he also had 32 gunners. Lt. von Gruben of Regiment Borcke was placed in charge of the infantry. A second Battalion, under Stabskapitain von Arenstorff, was going to be formed, but its men were used to make up the losses suffered by the first at the Battle of Naugard (18 February). The cavalry consisted of two squadrons of dragoons under Lt. von Diezelsky of the King of Bavaria's Dragoons and Lt. Baron von Luetzow of the Cuirassier Regiment Reitzenstein, as well as two hussar squadrons under Lt. Elderhorst of the

Usedom Hussars and Lt. von Brünnow of the Rudorff Hussars. The corps continued to grow at quite a rapid rate, and recorded the following strength on 4 June:

Seven staff

Two squadrons Dragoons: eight officers, 22 NCOs, four trumpeters, two surgeons, 20 carabineers, 176 troopers, two farriers.

Two squadrons Hussars: seven officers, 22 NCOs, four trumpeters, two surgeons, 20 carabineers, 176 troopers, two farriers.

Musketeer of III.Btl., 9. Reserve-Infanterie-Regiment, July 1813. This man is wearing a British rifleman's dark green tunic with black facings, and yellow buttons. The shako also appears to be British. See Plate D2.

Detachment Mounted Jaegers: one officer, two NCOs, one bugler, 30 troopers.

Cavalry depot: one officer, four NCOs, 40 troopers.

Two companies Fusiliers: eight officers, 20 NCOs, 20 Schuetzen, 240 privates, two surgeons, five musicians.

Jaeger Company Otto: four officers, ten NCOs, three buglers, 200 men, one surgeon.

Light Artillery Detachment: two horse guns, two foot guns (a present from the king of Sweden).

The men of Schill's Freikorps consisted largely of veterans who had served with regiments such as the Prince of Orange's, Borcke, Braunschweig-Oels, Owstien, Pirch, Winning, Zenge, Puttkamer, Moellendorff, Arnim, Prince Ferdinand, Count Kunheim, Zastrow, etc. The troopers of the two dragoon squadrons were mainly from the Queen's and Prince William's Regiments, the hussars from Rudorff and Gettkandt.

On 27 November 1807 Schill was ordered to reorganise his infantry into a light battalion of four companies; and in August 1808, the 'Light Battalion von Schill' was used to form part of the Life Infantry Regiment. Jaeger Company Otto became part of the newly-raised Guard Jaeger Battalion in November 1808. On 8 April 1808 Schill's cavalry were ordered to wear hussar uniforms, and in September 1808, they became the 2nd Brandenburg Hussar Regiment von Schill. Schill's artillery was absorbed by the regular army.

At first, the uniforms and equipment of Schill's corps were so varied that it looked more like a gang of robbers than a military formation. The infantry had only a few muskets, and many men were armed with pikes or scythes. At the beginning of March 1807 they received supplies of Swedish muskets, followed in May by a delivery from Britain of sufficient size. The infantry were gradually equipped with shakos which had white and yellow trim, black plumes, and white cords with a tassel whose colour indicated the company; blue tailless jackets with a row of tin buttons, red collars and cuffs (the 2nd Bn. at first wore yellow); long grey trousers cut in the shape of a gaiter at the foot; and black belts. The cartridge boxes at first had a 'GR' badge, indicating their British origin, but they were soon replaced by the Royal Prussian monogram 'FWR'. The officers wore whatever they pleased, and carried British cavalry sabres in iron scabbards; in battle, they often used rifles.

The cavalry troopers at first wore their old uniforms, and were later supplied with items from the depots of the Queen's Dragoons, Baillodz and Reitzenstein Cuirassiers. Supplies of greatcoats and

Musketeer of II.Btl. 4. Reserve. Inf.-Regt., autumn 1813. This uniform was made in Britain for Portuguese troops but supplies were diverted to the Prussians: see Plate D1.

overalls (blue or grey) were obtained whenever possible. The mounted Jaegers wore green coatees with red collars and cuffs, and grey overalls with red stripes.

It was this Maj. von Schill who attempted to spark off a rebellion against the French in Northern Germany in 1809. He was killed on 31 May in Stralsund, and the uprising was crushed.

In Silesia:

Preparations for the defence of Silesia were begun only after the Battle of Jena and were thus rather rushed. Various volunteer formations were raised, including a National Jaeger Corps in Schweidnitz; a Schuetzen Company under Lt. von Reichmeister of Boguslawski's Fusilier Battalion; and a Jaeger Company under Lt. Ehrenberg of the Field Jaeger Regiment, which consisted of professional huntsmen. As the campaign in the province progressed, a number of other formations were raised—see below.

Napoleon entrusted his brother Jerome with the task of conquering Silesia and gave him three divisions of his German allies to accomplish this task, namely Divisions Deroy and Wrede (Bavarians) and one of Wuerttembergers, a total of 23,000 men. He took the fortress of Glogau after a short siege and a two-day bombardment, and then moved on to besiege Breslau, the capital of Silesia. The Prussians had had some time to prepare themselves: the population of this city was behind the garrison, and there was a determination not to let this fortress fall into French hands. Breslau held out until 16 February 1807. A number of attempts were made to relieve the garrison, and the besiegers were constantly harassed by units and Freikorps under the overall command of the Prince of Anhalt-Pless. One of these was the Detachment (or Freikorps) Stoessel, consisting of three squadrons of cavalry and five companies of Schuetzen along with four falkonettes.

The garrisons of Glatz and Silberberg were supported by a number of light infantry and cavalry units. The former eventually grew to 12 companies in strength, the latter to ten squadrons. The infantry were divided into six divisions, each of two companies. The 1st Division consisted of Schuetzen Companies Polczinski and Reichmeister. Their uniforms were dark blue jackets with short tails, red collars, cuffs and facings; blue trousers with red piping; and tricorns with a white feather plume. The 2nd Division consisted of Jaeger Companies Guentz and Offeney; due to losses sustained at the battle of Adelsbach on 15 May, they were amalgamated with Companies Franckenberg and Blacha. Their uniforms consisted of green jackets with black collars and cuffs, grey trousers and shakos. The 3rd Division consisted of Jaeger Companies Stengel and Freyburg. Their uniforms were dark green coatees with green collars and cuffs, grey trousers, and grey shakos with a green feather plume. The 4th Division (Lt. von Gayl) consisted of Grenadier-Jaeger-Company Sell and Fusilier Com-

Part of a picture taken from a regimental history showing the various uniforms worn by members of that regiment from 1813 to 1905. Of particular interest are the three figures on the left. The officer (*far left*) is wearing the regulation Line uniform; the NCO (*next left*) is wearing the Portuguese uniform supplied during the summer of 1813, while the musketeer is wearing the grey reserve uniform issued in spring 1813. The reserve regiments wore several different uniforms, sometimes simultaneously.

Silesian militiamen, August 1813: see Plate D3.

pany Clausewitz. They wore 'steel green' jackets with black collars and facings, and grey trousers; Coy. Sell had grenadier caps, Coy. Clausewitz shakos. The 5th Division consisted of Jaeger Companies Berswordt and Ingenheim, and they wore green jackets with black (Ingenheim green) collars and facings, grey trousers and shakos. The 6th Division consisted of Jaeger Companies Vaerst and Count Schoenaich. Vaerst wore green jackets with black collars and cuffs, grey trousers and felt helmets; Schoenaich wore light green coatees with facings and collars of the same colour, grey trousers, and shakos with a green plume. Field Jaeger Company Ehrenberg had green jackets with a yellow shoulder band, red collars and facings, green overalls, and tricorns with a green plume.

Manteuffel's cavalry squadron were known as the 'Grenadiers à Cheval' because they wore grenadier caps with their dragoon uniforms. However, from May, as they were constantly mistaken for enemy cavalry, they were re-equipped with dark blue hussar dolmans with yellow collars. Squadrons Stoessel, Schill and Biberstein had blue pelisses with white piping; Kleist, dark blue with black; and Haxthausen, green with white. They all had grey trousers, and white feather plumes on their shakos. Witowsky wore the brown uniforms of Regiment Prince Pless. Uhlan Squadron Gayl had dark blue tunics of the same cut as the Austrian uhlans with crimson facings, and dark blue and crimson chequered pennants.

Although a number of Silesian fortresses fell to the French and their allies, the Prussian flag still flew over the fortresses of Cosel, Glatz and Silberg at the end of the war. In recognition of their performance, a number of the provisional and Freikorps units which fought in this campaign were taken into the reorganised Prussian Army. Grenadier Battalion Losthin became the Silesian Grenadier Battalion. The light infantry became the Silesian Schuetzen Battalion, and the Fusilier Battalion of the 2nd Silesian Infantry Regiment. The 2nd Silesian Hussar Regiment and the Life Uhlan Squadron were formed from the cavalry units mentioned above.

The Campaigns of the Wars of Liberation (1813–15)

The word 'foreigner', when used in the context of the Brandenberg-Prussian Army should be interpreted with great care. Europe is a continent which contains a number of nationalities which have spread over large areas during the course of the centuries: intermixing was, and still is, common. Moreover, political boundaries did not, and sometimes still do not, correspond to linguistic and national divisions. Prussia itself was a central European state whose territories were spread over a wide area with a number of dispersed enclaves. The main mass of Brandenburg-Prussia is spread over parts of what are now Germany, Poland, Russia and Czechoslovakia, so to take the word 'foreigner' here to mean 'non-German' is quite wrong. A Polish-speaking Catholic peasant was just as much a native of Prussia as a German-speaking Lutheran resident of Berlin. However, a German-speaking Lutheran resident of Hanover was a 'foreigner'. There were a number of these so-called 'foreigners' in the Prussian Army who were as loyal to the Prussian crown as any native Brandenburger, and who were good German partriots anxious to rid their country of French domination. Furthermore, such Germans who were not already in the Prussian armed forces were often a ready source of manpower in time of war, and there were many willing recruits in the National Uprising of 1813. They were used to form a number of Freikorps. There were also a number of so-called 'foreign' formations which fought side by side with Prussian units, often in the same brigades and corps. Some of

Peaked cap of the Pomeranian Militia, 1813–15. This item, in the Museum for German History in Berlin, is blue with a white band and piping; the tin Landwehr cross is sewn in place.

This flag was carried by a battalion of the Silesian Militia from Segan: the inscription reads 'Saganer Kreis' (District of Sagan).

these units consisted of genuine volunteers; others were not quite so willing and enthusiastic.

The most famous of the Freikorps of the Wars of Liberation (1813–15) was that raised by Maj. von Luetzow, who had fought alongside Schill. He was given permission to form his Corps in February 1813, and initially recruited from inhabitants of those former Prussian territories west of the River Elbe which Prussia had lost in 1807. By the middle of March he had raised four companies of infantry and two squadrons of cavalry. The majority of his recruits were artisans and peasants, and many were a mere 17 years old. Perhaps not of great military value, Luetzow's Freikorps has, however, been the subject of many poems, songs and historical novels. On 17 June 1813, shortly after the start of the armistice, this Corps was attacked by the French and all but wiped out. Recruiting during the summer armistice more than made up for this, and by the middle of August Luetzow's Freikorps had grown to three battalions of infantry (with a company of Tyrolese sharpshooters in the 2nd Bn.), three detachments of volunteer Jaegers, two squadrons of hussars, two of uhlans and one of volunteers, as well as a battery of artillery. The total strength of the Corps at this time was around 3,600 men. In the reorganisation of March 1815 Luetzow's men were used to form the 25th Infantry Regt., the 6th Uhlans, and part of the 9th Hussars.

Luetzow's Freikorps had, and in some circles still has a good deal of romantic appeal. It had a reputation for great daring, and Luetzow himself was wounded a number of times. Moreover, it attracted all sorts of intellectuals, artists and poets, to the extent that its members seem sometimes to have spent much of their time writing verse and composing songs! Two of its most famous members were Theodor Koerner, a Saxon who met a

The reverse of the previous flag. The original inscription reads: 'Mitt Gott fuer Koenig und Vaterland', which was the motto of the Landwehr. It is interesting to note that a further inscription has been added at a later date, reading: 'Unter der Anfuehrung des braven General von Dobschuetz focht ruhmvoll unter dieser Fahne das tapfere Sagan Landwehr Batallion bey (?), Dennewitz, Juetebog(?), Dessau und Wittenberg'. Translated, it reads: 'Under the leadership of the brave General von Dobschuetz (a commander in the IV Prussian Corps), the bold Sagan Landwehr Battalion fought with glory at (?), Dennewitz, Juetebog(?), Dessau and Wittenberg'. The militia were not allowed to have flags, but this item in the Museum for German History would seem to indicate that not only was this flag carried, but also preserved, and inscribed at a later date.

premature death, and Max von Schenckendorf, whose works are studied by students of German literature even today. Another famous member of the Corps, although for different reasons, was a lady by the name of Eleonore Prochaska, who disguised herself as a man so that she would be accepted in the Corps; she died when hit by a French ball at the battle on the Goehrde (16 September 1813), supposedly while beating a captured French drum, and confessed her deception to her lieutenant at the moment of death.

At this point, it would be convenient to explain the difference between a 'volunteer' and a 'volunteer Jaeger'. There were a good many volunteers in the free and foreign formations, but only a few of these came from families which were sufficiently wealthy to provide their sons with their own uniform, weapon and equipment. Those volunteers who equipped themselves were designated 'Jaeger', a title which bore some prestige, and were grouped together in separate detachments so that they would not have to rub shoulders too often with the lower ranks of society. The word 'Jaeger' is one which does not lend itself too easily to translation into English, as there was no real equivalent in the British armed forces, so it has been left in its German form in this work.

Not as well known as Luetzow's Corps, but probably of greater military value, was the Mecklenburg-Strelitz Hussar Regiment, a unit of 'foreign' volunteers which fought in the campaigns of 1813 and 1814 as part of Yorck's Corps. This regiment was formed on the order of Duke Charles of Mecklenburg-Strelitz who was the father of Queen Louise, the late wife of the king of Prussia. The unit performed so well that the king of Prussia presented it with a standard in 1815. It was four squadrons strong, with 20 officers, 44 NCOs, 12 buglers and 400 troopers. It also had a detachment of 60 volunteer Jaegers. The uniform was black (green for the Jaegers) with yellow cords.

Kapitain von Reiche formed a 'Foreign Jaeger Battalion' from volunteers in Berlin and later on the Lower Elbe. They wore a green Jaeger uniform with green shoulder straps, and were armed with infantry muskets; the volunteer Jaegers had rifles.

Lt.Col. von Reuss was given permission to form a unit of 'foreigners'. The 1st Bn. was formed in Berlin in April 1813, the 2nd in May. From 5 July this unit

Flag of the Berlin Landsturm, 3rd Coy., 24th Battalion. White field, black eagle and cross, blue scroll, gold lettering.

was called the 'Elbe Infantry Regiment'. It was joined by a 3rd Bn. in October 1813; and became the 26th Infantry Regt. in the reorganisation of March 1815.

In May 1813 Major von Hellwig was given command of the 3rd and 4th Sqns. and some volunteers of the 2nd Silesian Hussar Regt., and was sent off to conduct partisan operations behind enemy lines. A third squadron was raised in Berlin, and about 100 foot soldiers also joined the Corps. During the armistice of summer 1813 the Corps was clothed in uniforms sent from Britain. The cavalry received red dolmans and pelisses which had white cords. For headwear, they had fur colpacks. The front rank were armed with lances. In October and November a strong squadron of volunteer Jaegers was formed in the Halberstadt area, and the infantry were brought up to battalion strength— three companies and a Jaeger detachment. The infantry were clothed in green English Rifle uniforms. In March 1815 the 27th Infantry Regt. was formed from Reiche's Battalion, Hellwig's Infantry and the Reserve Battalion of the Elbe Infantry Regiment.

Maj. von Schill, a brother of the Schill of 1809 fame, took a detachment of 100 of the 2nd Silesian Hussars to join the Russian Col. von Tettenborn in Hamburg. With royal permission, he raised two squadrons of hussars, there; they wore blue uniforms with yellow cords.

The so-called 1st Thuringian Battalion was formed from a provisional battalion raised on Napoleon's order to replace the 4th Confederation of the Rhine Regt. which formed part of the garrison of the besieged city of Danzig. On 13 April 1813, it was taken prisoner by a detachment of 15 hussars and mounted Jaegers from the 1st Silesian Hussar Regt., and joined the Prussian Army. It gained new recruits from German prisoners-of-war and deserters. It fought in the autumn campaign of 1813 as the 2nd Fusilier (Light) Bn. of the Life Regt., part of Horn's Brigade in Yorck's Corps. The battalion was disbanded in 1814. This unit is particularly interesting and unusual: it wore French-style uniforms, and drilled according to the French regulations, yet it fought, and fought well, as part of the Prussian Army.

After Napoleon's first abdication in 1814 a number of 'foreign' units joined the Prussian Army. These were organisations which had either been part of other armies, or which had been raised in areas which had since come under Prussian control. One such unit was the 'German Legion', formerly the 'Russo-German Legion', which became part of the Prussian Army on 2 June 1814.

This unit had been raised from 1812 in Russia, firstly from German prisoners-of-war and deserters, and later from just about anybody available. The Legion formed part of Wallmoden's Corps on the Lower Elbe in 1813, and eventually reached a strength of seven infantry battalions, one company of Jaegers, two regiments of hussars, and two horse batteries. In 1814 the Legion fought in the Netherlands. A number of Prussian officers joined the Legion in 1812, and many of the early recruits were from the Prussian Army: for instance, the Legion's Jaeger Bn. was recruited from members of the East Prussian Jaegers. The collapse of the Grande Armée provided a source of new recruits throughout 1812, and the desertion of various allies of the French in the 1813 campaign allowed the formation of new battalions and the replacement of losses. In the reorganisation of March 1815 the infantry of the Legion were used to form the 30th and 31st Infantry Regts., and the cavalry were combined to form Uhlan Regt. No. 8.

Berg was a further area which came under Prussian administration. From the end of 1813 this district provided the Prussian Army with one battalion of grenadiers, two regiments of Line infantry (one of three battalions and one of two), four companies of volunteer Jaegers, one hussar regiment of five squadrons (the first being volunteers), one foot and half a horse battery. As only a few men had survived the Russian campaign most of these were raw recruits. The remnants of the famous Berg Lancer Regt. joined the new hussar regiment. Berg's resources of manpower were so exhausted that there was no one left to join the militia which was being formed; instead, the Berg Militia was recruited from enclaves of Berg territory elsewhere in north-western Germany. These troups joined the V German Army Corps under the Duke of Saxe-Cobourg, and participated in the siege of Mainz in 1814. In March 1815 the two infantry regiments were consolidated in the Prussian Line as Infantry Regts. Nos. 28 and 29. Hussar Regt. No. 11 was formed from three squadrons of Berg Hussars, while the 2nd Sqn. of the Hussars became part of the 5th Uhlan Regiment.

The Militia

The Prussian Landwehr or Militia is often seen as a new phenomenon which originated in the 'People's War' of 1813. However, the roots of the Prussian militia lay further back, and this post-Jena reform, as so many others, was already being considered before 1806. Frederick the Great raised a militia in the heartlands of his kingdom at a time of great need during the Seven Years' War. The partition of Poland towards the end of the 18th century had brought Brandenburg-Prussia into closer contact with two larger, richer and more powerful neighbours, namely Russia and Austria. Prussia's limited resources of manpower would need to be utilised more efficiently if she were to face either or both of these powers in a war; and plans for the formation of militia to back up the army were considered. Minister von Schroetter published a memorandum on this subject in 1799; Col. von Phull mentioned such an idea in a memorandum dated 12 November 1800; and the Duke of Brunswick repeated such ideas during his examination of the defences of Brandenburg-Prussia's

Freikorps, 1806/07:
1, 2: Infantrymen, Von Schill's Freikorps
3: Light infantryman, Kalckreuth's Freikorps

A

Freikorps, 1806/07:
1, 2: Officer & Grenadier Jaeger,
     Grenadier Jaeger Co. von Sell
3: Grenadier, 'Brown' Gren. Bn. von Losthin

B

Reserve infantry, spring 1813:
1: Musketeer, 1st Reserve Bn., 1st W. Prussian Inf. Regt.
2: Musketeer, 2nd Reserve Bn., 1st W. Prussian Inf. Regt.
3: Musketeer, 3rd Bn., 1st E. Prussian Inf. Regt.

C

Reservists & Militia, autumn 1813:
1: Reservist, 2nd Bn., 4th Reserve Inf. Regt.
2: Reservist, 3rd Bn., 9th Reserve Inf. Regt.
3: Silesian Militiaman

D

Militia, 1813-15:
1: Officer, Silesian Militia, autumn 1813
2: Militiaman, 1815
3: Officer, Westphalian Militia, 1815

E

'Foreign' formations, 1813-15:
1: Private, Thuringian Bn., autumn 1813
2: Berg Grenadier, 1814
3: Infantryman, Russo-German Legion, 1812-14

1

2

3

'Foreign' troops & Freikorps, 1813-15:
1: Hussar, 1st Hussar Regt., Russo-German Legion, 1812-15
2: Gunner, Horse Artillery, Russo-German Legion
3: Infantryman, Hellwig's Raiding Corps, 1813

G

'Foreign' troops & Freikorps, 1813-15:
1: Hussar, Hellwig's Raiding Corps, 1813
2: Jaeger, Luetzow's Freikorps, 1813-15
3: Musketeer, Inf. Regt. No. 28, 1815

H

eastern frontier in the early years of the 19th century.

The battalions of militia raised would be attached to the Line formations, trained by good NCOs and commanded by retired officers. Ruechel and Knesebeck pressed the king to adopt such plans: several years before Jena and Auerstedt, a number of so-called 'conservative' officers were urging their monarch to establish a 'nation in arms'. Discussions continued until the mobilisation of 1805 disrupted these attempts to reorganise the army, and the war of 1806/7 stopped the introduction of many planned reforms. After the Peace of Tilsit such plans were mooted again, but the Treaty of Paris forbade the formation of a militia. The founding of the Landwehr in Prussia finally occurred early in 1813 as a result of the uprising in East Prussia following the desertion of Yorck's Corps, and was in fact an act of rebellion rather than the realisation of long-considered plans.

Napoleon had compelled a reluctant Prussia to contribute a contingent to his ill-fated Russian Campaign in 1812. Yorck (see MAA 149 *Prussian Light Infantry 1792–1815* for a short biography of this famous general) became the commander of the Prussian Auxiliary Corps; and when the opportunity presented itself, he declared his contingent neutral and joined the Russians in taking over East Prussia. This province was therefore in a state of war with France while the remainder of the kingdom was still officially her ally. East Prussia needed to raise all available manpower, and plans for the formation of a militia were put into motion as soon as possible. On 7 February 1813 the East Prussian Landwehr was founded: it was planned to put 20,000 militiamen in the field, and to form a reserve of 10,000. Every man between the ages of 18 and 45 was liable for service unless he was a priest or a teacher; some civil servants were also exempted.

Events moved quickly, and the whole of Prussia was soon at war with France. On 17 March 1813 a decree founding a militia throughout Prussia was issued. For this purpose, the monarchy was divided into four military districts, namely:
1) The area between the Elbe and Oder, excluding Silesia.
2) Silesia.
3) The area between the Oder and Vistula, excluding Silesia.

4) The area between the Vistula and the Russian border.

Recruits were to be drawn from all fit men between the ages of 17 and 40, although efforts were made to exclude married men and those with dependents; in fact, the majority of recruits were under 25 years old. Infantry companies of 150–200 men were to be formed, as well as cavalry squadrons of 72–96 men. A battalion was to consist of four companies, and a brigade of four battalions. The four squadrons of cavalry in a brigade were to form a regiment. Each infantry company was to be divided into sections of 12 men under a corporal; and wherever possible, men of the same village or area were to be kept together. The cavalry squadrons were divided into sections of eight men. Each company was to have a captain, four lieutenants, one sergeant-major and two drummers; each squadron was to have a captain, two or three lieutenants, a sergeant-major and a bugler. Campaign conditions and local difficulties meant that this organisation was largely theoretical, and the information given here is only meant as a rough outline.

The uniform was to consist of a blue or black Litewka coat. The collar was to be in the provincial colour, and the four battalions within a brigade were to be distinguished by the colour of the shoulder straps: white, red, yellow and light blue. The number of the brigade was to be sewn on the shoulder strap in yellow (or in red in the third battalions). NCOs were to have black and white lace on the collar and cuffs; volunteers, a white band around the cuffs. Headwear was to be a blue cloth cap with a black leather peak and a band in the provincial colour. Further cap distinctions were to be the Prussian cockade (white with a black centre); and the 'Landwehr Cross', an 'Iron Cross' style of badge bearing the inscription 'Mit Gott fuer Koeing und Vaterland' ('With God for King and Fatherland'). The actual uniforms worn varied enormously, and some examples are included in the plates. The provincial colours of the earliest militia formations were as follows:
East Prussia—poppy red with white buttons.
Kurmark and Neumark—poppy red with yellow buttons.
West Prussia—black with white buttons.
Pomerania—white with yellow buttons.

Silesia—yellow with white buttons.

After the Battle of Leipzig in October 1813, Napoleon was driven out of Germany and new areas for recruitment were made available to the Prussians. The militia raised in these areas had the following provincial colours;
Westphalia—green with white buttons.
Elbe District—light blue with yellow buttons.
Rhineland—madder red with yellow buttons.

As a temporary measure, due to the shortage of firearms, the front rank of the militia infantry were armed with 8½ft-long pikes while the second and third ranks were armed with muskets. It is possible that some militia formations took to the field in autumn 1813 partially armed with pikes, but as so many men dropped out of the ranks exhausted in the early marches of the campaign, it is likely that the pikes were quickly replaced with their firearms. Moreover, the first successful battles of the

campaign provided supplies of French muskets which were not wasted. NCOs were to have a short sword in addition to their muskets, and the men were also to carry axes or spades. The cavalry troopers were to be armed with lances, sabres and pistols. Experience was to show that the decision to arm the militia cavalry with lances, imitating the Cossacks, was perhaps not such a good idea because they lacked the necessary skills to use them properly.

Initially, the militia were trained two days a week (on Sundays and Wednesdays) so as not to disrupt the economy too much. Once their equipment arrived, they were trained in companies for a week, in battalions for a further two weeks, and then in brigades. The individual militiaman was trained to use his firearm or pike; the units were trained to manoeuvre and to form the attack column. The third ranks were trained to act as skirmishers. A shortened and revised version of the 1812 Regulations were used.

A contemporary caricature of the Berlin Landsturm: rather a rabble to be carrying flags like the one in the previous picture!

On 27 July 1813, as the armistice was drawing to an end, the militia were formed into regiments, ready to take the field. By this time, the following formations had been raised:

	Inf. Regts.	Cav. Regts.	Bns.	Sqns.
East Prussia:	5	5	20	16
West Prussia:	3	3	11	9
Pomerania:	3	3	12	12
Neumark:	3	2	12	8
Kurmark:	7	7	26	28
Silesia:	17	10	68	40

Once hostilities recommenced there were numerous reorganisations and amalgamations of units, so the above table gives only an impression of the size of the militia. About 120,000 men had been raised for service in the militia, and the entire army consisted of just over 270,000 men, so the militia formed a significant part of the forces available to Prussia.

Losses to the militia formations were particularly high. For example, of the 24 battalions of Silesian militia in Yorck's Corps, only sufficient men remained after the battle of Moeckern on 17 October 1813 to form seven weak battalions. Of the 13,369 militiamen Yorck had at the beginning of the campaign, only 2,164 reached the Rhine. The early marches took their toll: the weaker men soon became fatigued and dropped out. Supply problems meant that during the retreat into Silesia in August 1813 many Silesian militiamen were driven by hunger into returning to their homes, greatly reducing the numbers available in the field. Once battle was joined losses could be high, as inexperienced troops were prone to wild charges and panic-stricken retreats. The militia learned much of the art of war from first-hand experience, however, and by the later battles of the autumn campaign they were as much veterans as the Line troops, and every bit as dependable.

Once Germany had been liberated further recruitment areas were made available to the Prussian Army. A new Military District was created between the Elbe and the Weser. Here, three militia infantry regiments of four battalions and one cavalry regiment of four squadrons were raised. The Mansfeld Pioneer Battalion, four companies strong, was formed from miners and workers in associated industries: it was regarded as being a militia formation. In the Military District between the Weser and the Rhine five militia infantry regiments were raised, and a cavalry regiment of six squadrons. The Elbe Landwehr participated in the siege of Madgeburg, while part of the Westphalian Landwehr followed Buelow's Corps into the Netherlands.

In 1815 eight Rhineland militia infantry and two and a half cavalry regiments were raised, although these never saw action. Further militia units were raised in Prussia's other new districts.

The Landwehr of 1813–15 was very much an improvised militia consisting largely of young men. New regulations were issued in 1814 and came into effect after the Napoleonic Wars: the new Landwehr was no longer a militia, but was to be a reserve for the regular army consisting of trained men who had served their time, but who could be

Fichte, the famous German philosopher, as a Landsturm man.

called up in time of war. In fact, the post-Waterloo Landwehr was rather similar to the 'Kruemper' of the Napoleonic Wars.

The final line of Prussia's defences at this time was the Landsturm, which was roughly the equivalent of the British Home Guard of the Second World War. The Landsturm was a local defence force consisting of all the remaining male population capable of fighting. Their rôle was to defend their villages against the French, to round up stragglers and deserters, and to hinder the movement of supplies by the enemy. The Landsturms saw action on a number of occasions.

Some historians tend to see the Landwehr as having little military value, and as a consequence

Contemporary aquatint by Genty of a militiaman in France in 1815: see Plate E2.

LANDWEHR
de la Poméranie

Prussia's militia tends to be held in low regard. The blame for such an opinion of the Landwehr cannot, however, be laid entirely at the feet of later historians, because many contemporaries had a low opinion of this militia too, especially before it had proved itself in battle. Yorck wrote a letter on 4 July 1813 in which he stated: 'The First Army Corps has undergone great changes. It now consists entirely of recruits; I haven't so many as 1,000 old soldiers. To make matters worse, I have been given four of the worst militia battalions'.

This lack of training was not helped by poor equipment, as illustrated by this quote from the diary of the 13th Silesian Landwehr Regt. (part of Yorck's Corps): 'On these forced marches [i.e. in August 1813] the consequences of the extremely poor clothing of the militia became apparent. Largely without greatcoats, in simple linen trousers, barefoot since their shoes had come off in the bottomless mud—even with the best will and with the strongest constitution, how could these poor militiamen, being quite unaccustomed to such exertion, put up with this? It was three days since they last had more than a mouthful of bread, as the damp spoiled the small stocks; there was even less brandy, too little to give the soldiers a ration. Filthy, exhausted, many fell to the ground, and more still would die as they had to stay behind in hospital, sick with fever'.

One can see why Yorck was not pleased to have his already stretched supply system further burdened by large numbers of inexperienced troops who would quickly fall sick. However, once the Landwehr went into battle, they soon proved themselves, as the following quotations show. The first, from Droysen's biography of Yorck, refers to battle of Loewenberg on 21 August 1813:

'. . . Yorck sent the 2nd Brigade into the battle to prevent, for as long as possible, the enemy from breaking out of Plagwitz and on to the Goldenberg road. It was the first time that the militia came under fire; their performance was above all expectations, and they fought like old Line troops—particularly the Schweidnitz Battalion [5th Silesian Landwehr Infantry Regt.] which was part of the vanguard. It attacked the enemy twice with the bayonet as he was breaking out of Plagwitz, and threw him back into the village. As the unit was falling back in good order under canister fire to its position, an adjutant asked its leader, a Capt. Kossecki, why he was fighting in line instead of sending skirmishers out against the enemy. Kossecki answered that as a former fusilier [light infantryman] he did know what to do; but it was the first time that the battalion had been under fire, and if he was to break it up by sending out skirmishers, he did not have enough experienced officers to keep order, and he would rather die on the spot than see his battalion fall apart. When the battalion had used up all its ammunition it was withdrawn, and Yorck ordered the troops it passed by to form up and salute.' Yorck's opinion of the Landwehr had changed rapidly.

Finally, in a letter written shortly after the battle of Wartenburg (3 October 1813), Gneisenau described the rôle of the Prussian militia in the storm of the town of Wartenburg: 'The militia certainly played their part, particularly Battalion Sommerfeld from the Hirschberg District, which consisted largely of linen weavers. These young troops teach themselves how to fight. I only hope our commanders can make proper use of such a spirit in the army. "Look! This battalion of the Life Regiment is advancing against the enemy, they want to show that they are better than you", General Horn said to his militiamen. "No, no, we are just as good as them!" answered the militiamen, and at once they moved off against the enemy'. By October 1813, it would seem that the 'Landwehr' was considered every bit as good as the Line.

The militia which went to war in 1815 were largely similar in terms of experience and equipment to the old 'Landwehr' of August 1813, as many of the units present in the campaign in the Netherlands were newly raised, coming from Prussia's new territories in the west of Germany. Whatever these Westphalian militiamen lacked by way of training and clothing, they made up for in spirit. Hungry, and drenched by torrential rain, battalions of the Westphalian militia marched through deep mud for several hours before engaging Napoleon's élite Guardsmen in the struggle for Plançenoit, the key village in the rear of Napoleon's battle-line at Waterloo. The village changed hands several times. Undaunted by defeat, the Westphalians rallied and attacked again and again. This action was a fitting epitaph to the Landwehr.

The Battle on the Goehrde, 16 September 1813

The campaign on the Lower Elbe, although a sideshow when compared with events in Saxony, is nevertheless interesting, especially as a number of the formations covered in this work were involved in it. The Allied forces were commanded by Wallmoden and the French forces by Davout. The Allies' objective was to keep Davout bottled up in Hamburg as much as possible, and to make sure he did not interfere with the course of events in the main theatre, Saxony. Davout's objective was to keep Hamburg and Northern Germany in French hands, to ensure Denmark remained in alliance with France, and to pose a threat to the communications of the Army of the North under the Crown Prince of Sweden. Davout had the larger army, but had to maintain various garrisons. He also had less cavalry than Wallmoden, and thus the extent of any offensive operations he undertook was limited. Prior to the battle on the Goehrde, Wallmoden's only real success in that campaign, there had been a number of minor clashes and skirmishes in the course of the month of September.

Early in September Davout retreated into his prepared position in Ratzeburg where the Allied pursuit halted. This sudden withdrawal by Davout puzzled Wallmoden, who assumed that it was caused by the defeats suffered by the French in Saxony. Moreover, it seemed likely that Davout was going to move on Madgeburg—which at this time had a French garrison—and join up with Napoleon's main army. Wallmoden consequently moved part of his corps to Doemitz on 5 and 6 September to prepare a bridgehead, and from there to observe Davout's possible crossing points at Winsen and Harburg from the left bank of the Elbe. However, the thought of moving to Madgeburg had not crossed Davout's mind; so Wallmoden marched to Hagenow on 10 September. Here, he learned from papers captured by Cossacks from a French courier that part of the French 50th Division under Gen. Pécheux would be crossing the Elbe in the next few days to clear the left bank of Allied partisans, and thereby re-establishing communications with Madgeburg.

Acting on this information, Wallmoden moved the troops he had at Hagenow to Doemitz. By the evening of 14 September he had concentrated 9,000 infantry, 3,200 cavalry and 38 guns there. That evening, he received reports that Pécheux had actually crossed the Elbe. During the night Wallmoden followed suit, and moved to Dannenberg. By the evening of 14 September Pécheux had reached Lueneburg with 3,000 infantry, 80 cavalry and six guns. His orders were to drive Wallmoden's troops out of Dannenberg, thereby re-establishing direct communications between Hamburg and Madgeburg.

Pécheux continued his advance on 15 September despite the fact that he was constantly harassed by Cossacks. That afternoon he took up a position on the Steinker Hill (see map); one battalion covered the Goehrde Hunting Lodge (Jagdschloss), and

pickets were pushed out to the edge of the wood.

On 16 September Wallmoden hid his troops, hoping to ambush the French on the march. The afternoon passed without a sign of them, and it seemed likely that Pécheux knew what Wallmoden had in mind. He decided to go and find the French and attack them—rather a daring decision as Davout could have been setting a trap for him. If Davout was to move his troops up the right bank of the Elbe, Wallmoden's line of retreat would be cut.

The orders-of-battle of the armies involved were as follows:

French
Commander: Gen. Pécheux
Brigade Mielzynski:
3rd Line Regt. (4 bns.)
105th Line Regt. (1 bn.)

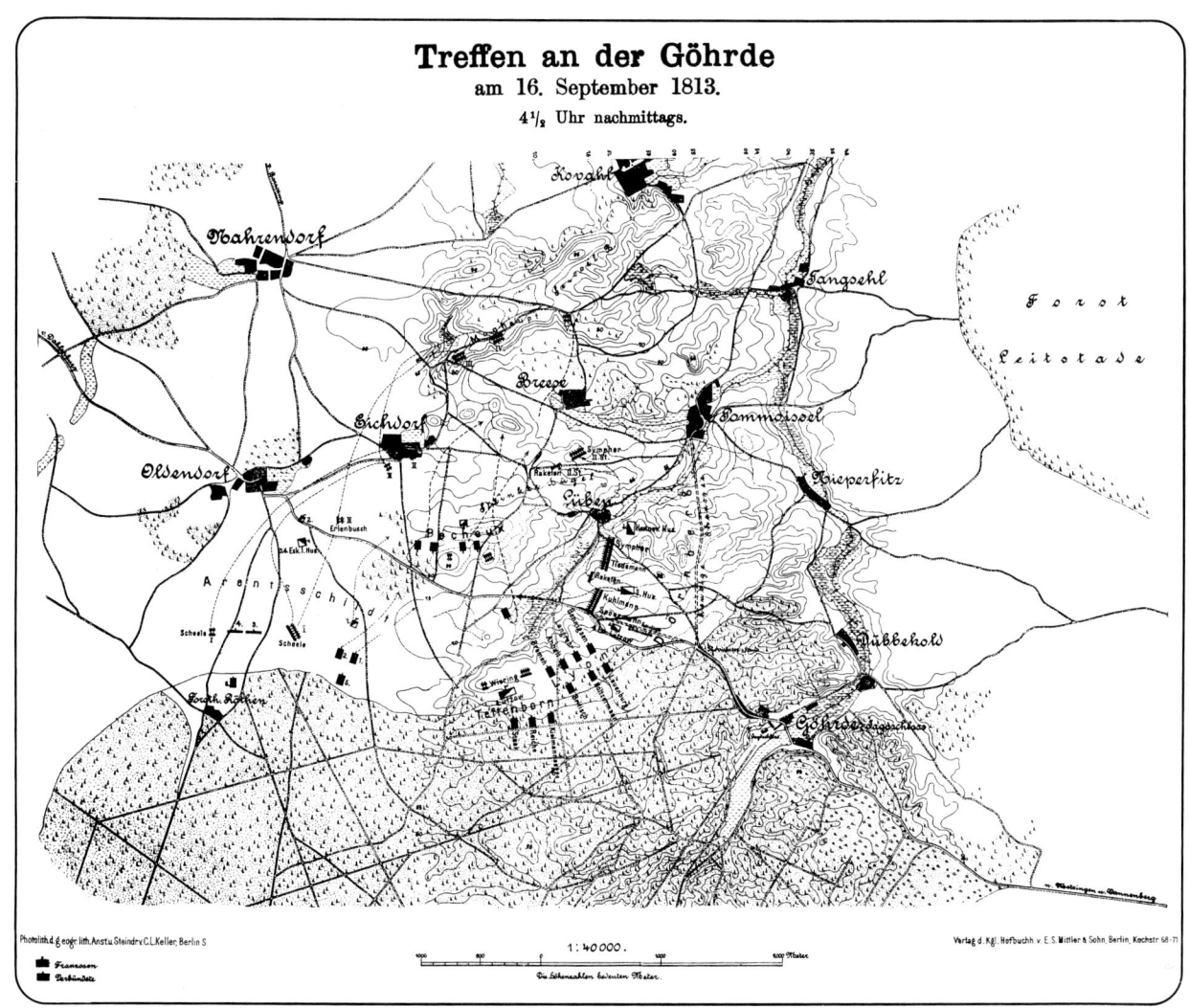

Treffen an der Göhrde
am 16. September 1813.
4½ Uhr nachmittags.

1 horse bty. (6 guns)
1 coy. 28th Chasseurs à Cheval

The East Prussian Militia storm Leipzig towards the end of that great battle. Note that the officer in the foreground is wearing the Litewka coat like his men instead of the regulation offficers' long-tailed coatee.

Allies

Vanguard: Gen. von Tettenborn
1 bn. Luetzow
1 bn. Reiche
½ bn. Kielmansegge (incl. Russo-German Jaeger)
5 sqns. Luetzow
Bty. Spoormann (Hanseatic)
Cossack Regts. Komisarow, Denisow, Sulin.

Division Gen. von Arentschildt
6 bns. Russo-German Legion
1st Hussar Regt. Russo-German Legion (4 sqns.)
1st. Horse bty. Russo-German Legion (8 guns)

Division Gen. Lyon
4 bns. Hanoverians
1 bn. Anhalters
1 bn. 73rd Foot (British)
½ bn. Holtzermann
Foot Bty. Wiering (6 guns)

Reserve Cavalary & Artillery: Gen. von Doernberg
3rd KGL Hussar Regt. (5 sqns.)
Lueneburg Hussars (2 sqns.)
Bremen-Verden Hussars (1 sqn.)
KGL Artillery (12 guns)
2nd Bty. Russo-German Legion (8 guns)
Rocket Detachment

Wallmoden formed his troops up into two columns and launched his attack. Column I consisted of Div. Arentschildt, and Column II— which he led personally—of the Vanguard and Div. Lyon. Column I was ordered to move up to the wood, then through it to the Roethen Lodge, then to the right to where the enemy was estimated to be and cut off his line of retreat. Column II was to move off an hour later to allow Column I to get into position. The infantry of the Vanguard were to move through the wood with Div. Lyon in support,

Bluecher and militiamen, autumn 1813. Note the various items of equipment carried by these militiamen.

while the Cossacks, cavalry and artillery were to go around the right of the wood and attack the enemy's flank.

Arentschildt started his movement at 12.15 pm and reached the near edge of the wood two hours later. It was another 7.5km to the Lodge. Wallmoden himself moved off at 1 pm. His movement was covered by the Cossacks, who chased off the French pickets very quickly, which resulted in the French losing contact with the Allies so that they had little idea of what Wallmoden was doing. At this time Wallmoden heard cannonfire coming from the direction that he would have expected if Davout was attacking along the right bank of the Elbe. He feared that he was now in a precarious position, but it was too late to stop his own attack. The Goehrde Woods were taken after some resistance from the French, and Wallmoden could now see Pécheux's position. He was on top of a line of hills. The French had a clear line of fire; furthermore, their position was protected by a marshy stream which the cavalry and artillery could not cross. Pécheux's right flank was protected by a small pine wood.

The battalion of Luetzow's infantry pressed on, supported by the fire of Spoormann's artillery and followed by Reiche. Four squadrons of Luetzow's cavalry provided further support. The single French battalion to their front was thrown back. The Chasseurs supporting them were thrown back in disorder, but not before having some effect. Attempts to follow up were thrown back with great loss to Luetzow's cavalry, and Luetzow himself was badly wounded. His infantry used the time gained by this attack to rally and reform. This infantry and Reiche attacked the single French battalion again, hoping to push it back into the main French position; but they were too few in numbers for such a bold undertaking, and were thrown back into the wood—though managing to drag a French howitzer back with them.

At about 4 pm, almost simultaneously with the defeat of the first attacks, the remaining divisions appeared at the edge of the wood. Hearing the cannonfire, Lyon had moved his men up at the double, and they were out of breath: they needed a rest, so the artillery deployed and opened fire immediately. Arentschildt, too, was prompted to take rapid action on hearing the gunfire. He deployed a battery and had it open fire even though it was out of effective range. The physical effect of this fire was minimal, but the moral effect was considerable: the French now knew that both their flanks and rear were threatened. Pécheux ordered an immediate retreat, hoping to save as many men as he could, but he had to stop and face the threat from Doernberg's cavalry. Their attack was, however, totally unsuccessful as part of the cavalry got stuck in the marsh and the rest were driven back by the French artillery. All Doernberg had managed to do was slow down the French retreat.

At 5.30 pm Wallmoden ordered Lyon to attack with his infantry. The French battalions stood close together in five squares. Lyon's men virtually surrounded them, and it was impossible for the artillery to give them any supporting fire for fear of killing their own infantry. The French fought with the determination to be expected in such a

The Army of Silesia crossing the Rhine on 1 January 1814. The militiamen shown in the foreground of this picture marched from here to Paris.

desperate situation. When their squares were broken they continued to fight in rallying clumps. The Allies were forced back, and Pécheux took the opportunity to fall back towards Eichdorf.

While this close combat was going on, Bde. Wardenburg of Div. Arentschildt, together with a troop of hussars, moved up towards Eichdorf to cut off the enemy's line of retreat. The first wave of this attack pushed two companies of French infantry out of Oldendorf and pursued them towards Dahlendorf, but did not catch up with them, the hussars did so later, taking three officers and 113 men prisoner. However, this diversion gave Pécheux a better chance of escaping; and Monhaupt, commander of the Russo-German artillery, recognised this fact and quickly deployed four of his guns on the southern edge of Eichdorf. Pécheux saw that he was about to be cut off, and knew that the only option he had was to force a way out. He marched his men towards the guns, which were virtually unprotected. Monhaupt's four guns spat out so much canister that the French were forced to change the direction of their march to Breese. Arentschildt took full advantage of this, sending his infantry off in pursuit and attacking with his hussars. The French carried on fighting with great determination, but were forced together in such a small area that they could not use their firearms. Many were cut down, and about 500 were taken prisoner. Their cannon and waggons were captured. Only the fading light saved Pécheux: 2,000 of his men escaped. In all, he lost about 1,500 men, about half of whom were taken prisoner, together with one Eagle, six guns, 16 ammunition waggons and one field smithy. Wallmoden's men were too exhausted to pursue: they had lost 32 officers, 526 men and 306 horses.

Wallmoden's plan was clear and daring. He should really have wiped the French out as he outnumbered them four to one. Instead, half of the French escaped, beaten but still in good order. Wallmoden's lack of total success was due largely to the tactical inexperience of his commanders and the over-enthusiasm of his troops, who often attacked at the wrong time and place. Unco-ordinated attacks were made instead of the one co-ordinated advance which Wallmoden had planned and ordered. Pécheux's greatest mistake was to stand and fight. However, he cannot really be blamed for his lack of

knowledge of his enemy's dispositions: his 80 chasseurs were not going to gain much intelligence when pitted against over 3,000 enemy cavalry. His men fought well against massive odds.

Gneisenau

August Wilhelm Neithardt von Gneisenau was one of Prussia's leading reformers, and a most capable general who had the misfortune of being over-shadowed by various contemporaries. He is usually seen as the man who played second fiddle to Scharnhorst during the era of reforms, and second fiddle to Bluecher during the campaigns of the Wars of Liberation. Perhaps history is a little unfair to a man whose rôle was often crucial.

Born on 27 October 1760, he was the son of a Saxon lieutenant of artillery; his mother was the daughter of a captain of artillery. He was of rather humble origins, and had an unsettled youth. His first military service was with a regiment of Austrian hussars. After a short time he transferred to the service of the Margrave of Anspach as a cadet. In 1781 he became a sergeant. His regiment was taken prisoner at Yorktown during the War of the American Revolution, but the fortunate Neithardt was in Germany at the time, and the opportunity to get a commission came his way. If one wanted to get on as an officer at this time, one had to be of noble birth, so the ambitious Neithardt made sure that his commission was for one 'August Wilhelm Neithardt *von Gneisenau*': a double-barrelled name helped then as much as it does now. The sub-lieutenant was posted to the Rifle Regiment which was shortly to go off to America. Although the young Gneisenau was not directly involved in any fighting, as the war in America was now coming to a close, he avidly learned everything he could about modern warfare from the German officers who had served there. The lessons of this war are said to have influenced Gneisenau greatly: in particular, he noticed the importance of popular support for the army, and the new style of 'People's War'. He returned to Germany with a head full of ideas.

For young German officers wanting a good army career, the place to be at this time was in the

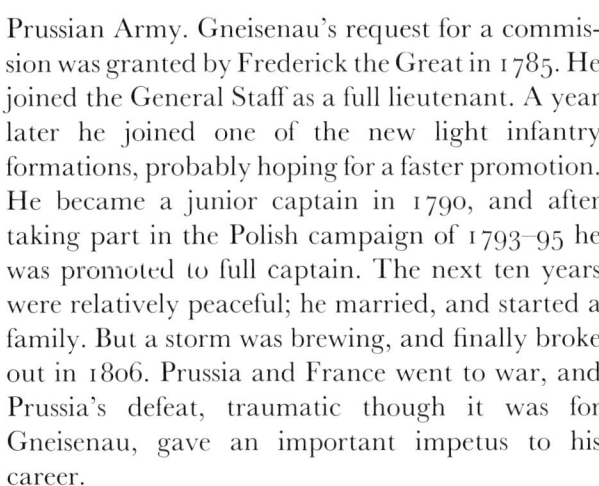

Contemporary painting of Gneisenau (*left*)—hardly as flattering as the later portrait (*right*): one wonders which is the more life-like.

Prussian Army. Gneisenau's request for a commission was granted by Frederick the Great in 1785. He joined the General Staff as a full lieutenant. A year later he joined one of the new light infantry formations, probably hoping for a faster promotion. He became a junior captain in 1790, and after taking part in the Polish campaign of 1793–95 he was promoted to full captain. The next ten years were relatively peaceful; he married, and started a family. But a storm was brewing, and finally broke out in 1806. Prussia and France went to war, and Prussia's defeat, traumatic though it was for Gneisenau, gave an important impetus to his career.

Slightly wounded at Saalfeld, Gneisenau was fortunate enough to escape from the battlefield of Jena unharmed. He made his way to the eastern provinces of the kingdom where a new Prussian army was assembling. He would carry the bitter taste of defeat in his mouth until the night of 18 June 1815 when, under his leadership, elements of the victorious Prussian Army pursued Bonaparte from the field of Waterloo with so much vigour that the French were not able to rally.

Gneisenau was commanded to raise a battalion, and promoted to major. The New Year found him in charge of a ragged collection of men, some in long coats, some in short tunics, some wearing hats, others with shakos. This battalion was to defend Danzig, achieve fame in Colberg, become part of the Royal Guard in recognition of its services, and finally to enter Paris, bringing down the Bonaparte dynasty.

Although Gneisenau's potential and talents had been recognised by his superiors, he did not enjoy public fame until his dramatic defence of the small fortress of Colberg on the Baltic coast of Pomerania. Gneisenau recognised the strategic importance of this port, as it was a point from which Britain could supply Prussia. He set about improving its defences and mobilising the population in support of the army. Gneisenau became a leader of a 'People's War'. The defence of Colberg is fascinating for any student of military history; sadly, lack of space prevents any detailed description of this episode here. Suffice to say that Colberg under Gneisenau held out until the end of the war, in sharp contrast to the shamefully rapid capitulations of so many

43

major Prussian fortresses in the wake of the defeats of October 1806.

Lt.Col. von Gneisenau was awarded the coveted *Pour le Mérite* in reward for his great achievement. In the war of 1806/7 he had shown himself to be a courageous soldier and a good commander of men in the field. He talents as a theoretician were going to be put to good use in the next period of Prussian history, as he was invited to join the Reorganisation Commission, the body that was going to reform the entire Prussian Army. Gneisenau may well have been overshadowed by Scharnhorst during this period, but his contribution should not be underestimated: he was one of that select handful of men who made Prussia into a modern state which would play an important rôle in the world for the next 150 years.

Between 1807 and the outbreak of war in 1813 Gneisenau did not rest; he channelled all his energies into preparations for war with France. His efforts were rewarded when he was appointed Quartermaster-General of the Army of Silesia under Bluecher's command. After Scharnhorst's premature death he became the Chief-of-Staff, and with Bluecher formed a team which was to be brilliantly successful in victory and doggedly resilient in defeat throughout the campaigns from August 1813 to June 1815. Gneisenau was the man who held the Prussian Army of the Lower Rhine together after the Battle of Ligny; Gneisenau was the man who organised its advance to the field of Waterloo; and Gneisenau was the man who led the pursuit after that fateful battle. He was one of that small number of great men who brought down Napoleon, changing the history of Europe and the world.

This French aquatint dated 1815 shows a Berg Grenadier (incorrectly labelled as a Saxon Grenadier of the Royal Prussian Guard—there never was such a thing!). It is interesting that even after the battle of Waterloo, members of what were by then the 28th and 29th Royal Prussian Infantry Regiments were wearing their old Berg uniforms.

Nº 6   Troupes Prussiennes   1815

GRENADIERS SAXONS

Réunis aux gardes royales Prussiennes en 1814.

The Plates

A: Freikorps units, 1806/7
The uniforms illustrated here are typical of those worn by these semi-regular units. They are a mixture of items of uniform from the soldiers' former regiment which have been retained, locally manufactured items replacing those damaged or worn out, and new items supplied to the unit. This plate is based on watercolours by Ludwig Scharf.

A1, A2: Infantry of Von Schill's Freikorps, 1807
It is a little difficult to determine exactly which units these men came from as their tunics are not readily identifiable as coming from a particular regiment. As Schill's men got their uniforms from anywhere and everywhere, it is perhaps a futile exercise trying to find any significance in the two different uniforms shown here. Note that the figure on the left is wearing long grey trousers cut in the shape of a gaiter at the foot. This style of trouser was introduced into the Prussian Army as a whole from 1815.

A3: Light infantryman of Kalckreuth's Freikorps

This is an interesting uniform: this Freikorps was supposed to be dressed in the uniform of Regt. Treskow, i.e. white facings, yet those worn by this light infantryman could not be more different. This is probably another local variation.

B: Freikorps units, 1806/7

The figures shown on Plate A were all based in the northern theatre of warfare, that is around Danzig, and their condition indicates the shortage of supplies there. These figures are of units founded in Silesia where the better-supplied fortresses and depots could provide the Freikorps with more uniform clothing. The above figures are based on plates from Knoetel's *Grosse Uniformenkunde*.

B1 & B2: Officer and Grenadier Jaeger, Grenadier-Jaeger Company von Sell, 1807

This unit was raised in the Silesian fortress of Glatz and formed part of its garrison. These men later joined the Fusilier (Light) Battalion of the 2nd Silesian Regt. after the best men had been selected for service in the Silesian Schuetzen Battalion.

B3: Grenadier, Brown Grenadier Battalion von Losthin

Due to shortage of cloth, the trousers and 'peach'-piped facings of this unit were made from brown cloth taken from the depot of a hussar regiment. This unit became the Silesian Grenadier Battalion in 1809, and in 1814 the Fusilier Battalion of the Kaiser Franz Grenadier Regiment.

C: Reserve Infantry, spring 1813

This plate is based on illustrations contained in various regimental histories.

C1: Musketeer, 1st Reserve Battalion, 1st West Prussian Infantry Regiment

A most interesting figure, probably a little untypical of the reserve units of spring 1813. Note that the grey tunic is cut in the same way as the blue tunics of the regulars, i.e. with tails, whereas the grey reservists' tunic (see C3) was supposed to be tailless.

C2: Musketeer, 2nd Reserve Battalion, 1st West Prussian Infantry Regiment

Another variation on the supposed norm. This man's entire uniform has been cut from blue cloth

Uniforms of Infantry Regiment No. 28. (*Left*) are the old white Berg uniforms faced light blue; (*right*) the new uniform introduced in 1815, which a few members of the regiment perhaps wore in the Waterloo campaign.

instead of grey. Note the canvas knapsack which was worn instead of the calfskin packs issued to the Line. Note also that a sword knot is worn tied around the sword belt, even though, due to the shortage of such side-arms, this man has not been issued with the infantry short sword itself.

C3: Musketeer, 3rd Battalion, 1st East Prussian Infantry Regiment

To an extent, the 'typical' reservists' uniform. This man is slightly better equipped than most as he is wearing a calfskin pack.

Plate D: Reservists and militia, autumn 1813

This plate shows that although by the autumn of 1813 the reservists were a little better equipped, the militia was in a poor state and hardly in a condition to take the field.

D1: Reservist, 2nd Battalion, 4th Reserve Infantry Regiment

This uniform was made in Britain and originally intended for her Portuguese allies. However, supplies were diverted to North Germany and to units of the Prussian Army. One can understand why such uniforms attracted ridicule. A blue grenade device was displayed on the white turnbacks.

D2: Reservist, 3rd Battalion, 9th Reserve Infantry Regiment

This uniform supplied by Britain was clearly made for the Rifles. It is not as garish as that shown as D1, and fitted in with those uniforms worn by a number of rifled-armed and volunteer units in the Prussian Army.

These two illustrations are based on watercolours produced in the mid-19th century of items in the Royal Prussian Arsenal in Berlin.

D3: Silesian militiaman

This figure can be regarded as a 'typical' Landwehr man of this time. The waxed-cloth cover to the peaked cap was common, and to some extent protected its wearer's head against the heavy rain which characterised that fateful autumn. This militiaman's shoes were probably lost in the deep mud through which he constantly had to march. Note the spoon he is carrying in his button hole. Based on contemporary accounts and illustrations.

E: Militia, 1813–15
E1: Officer, Silesian Militia, autumn 1813

This officer is somewhat better equipped than the infantryman shown on the previous plate. His uniform and equipment are virtually identical to that of a Line officer, and the only indication of militia status is his cap. Based on contemporary accounts and illustrations.

E2: Militiaman, 1815

This illustration is based on a plate by Genty in a contemporary series of the uniforms of the units occupying France after the battle of Waterloo: the original plate bears the caption 'Pomeranian Landwehr', but the red facings do not suggest Pomerania. Red was the provincial colour of East Prussia, the Neumark and the Kurmark. Note his calfskin knapsack; and the generally good condition of his clothing and equipment, in contrast to D3. Note also the veteran's medal he wears on his chest: this was given to participants in the campaigns of 1813–15 whose conduct had been meritorious. Note also the non-regulation white piping on the shoulder strap.

E3: Officer, Westphalian Militia, 1815

This officer is wearing the Litewka coat worn by most militia rankers. There are a number of contemporary illustrations showing this non-regulation practice by officers. Based on a mid-19th century watercolour of items in the Royal Prussian Arsenal in Berlin, and the Elberfeld Manuscript.

F: 'Foreign' formations, 1813–15
F1: Private, Thuringian Battalion, autumn 1813

This battalion wore a great variety of uniforms during its few months of service in the Prussian Army. Some of its members wore the uniforms issued by the various Saxon duchies they came from; others may not have been issued with a uniform at all until autumn 1813; and this man is wearing a mixture of Prussian and British items. The shako, belts, knapsack and side-arm are almost certainly Prussian; the tunic and greatcoat were manufactured in Britain. Based on a plate by Herbert Knoetel.

F2: Berg Grenadier, 1814

This French-style uniform was typical of that worn by a number of the states of the so-called 'Confederation of the Rhine'. This uniform would appear to have survived until after the battle of Waterloo, as a contemporary plate by Genty shows it being worn, slightly modified, during the occupation of France. Based on a plate in Richard Knoetel's *Grosse Uniformenkunde*; another source gives the shoulder straps as red.

F3: Infantryman, Russo-German Legion, 1812–14

A typical Russian uniform which was worn from 1812 to 1814, even when the Legion was in Prussian service. Based on a contemporary illustration in the Elberfeld Manuscript. There seem to be two rows of eight (?) brass buttons, and red piping, down the coatee front, and red lower edge piping. Blue collars distinguished the 2nd Bde., red the 1st; shoulder strap colours identified battalions.

G: 'Foreign' troops and Freikorps, 1813–15
G1: Hussar, 1st Hussar Regiment of the Russo-German Legion, 1812–15

This uniform was worn even after the hussars of the German Legion—as it was renamed in 1814—had been 'converted' into lancers for the 1815

An 1809 pattern Prussian musket. Although this particular musket was manufactured after the Napoleonic Wars, it was issued to one of the former Reserve Regiments: the stamps on the butt plate indicate musket no. 178 issued to the 4th Company (4C) of the 14th Infantry Regiment. (14.I.R.)

campaign. The old uniforms of all these non-Prussian units would appear to have been worn until the end of the Napoleonic Wars, if not longer. Based on the Elberfeld Manuscript.

G2: Gunner, Horse Artillery of the Russo-German Legion, 1815

The artillery of the Russo-German Legion was also taken into Prussian service, the horse artillery becoming Prussian Horse Batteries Nos. 18 and 19. Based on the Elberfeld Manuscript.

G3: Infantryman of Hellwig's Raiding Corps, 1813

This musket-armed infantryman is wearing the modified tunic of an English rifleman: a good number of these tunics would seem to have been sent to Prussia in 1813. The remainder of the uniform and equipment was probably Prussian in origin. Based on a plate by Richard Knoetel.

H: 'Foreign' troops and Freikorps, 1813–15
H1: Hussar of Hellwig's Raiding Corps, 1813

This uniform was also part of the large deliveries of equipment from Britain. These lance-armed cav-

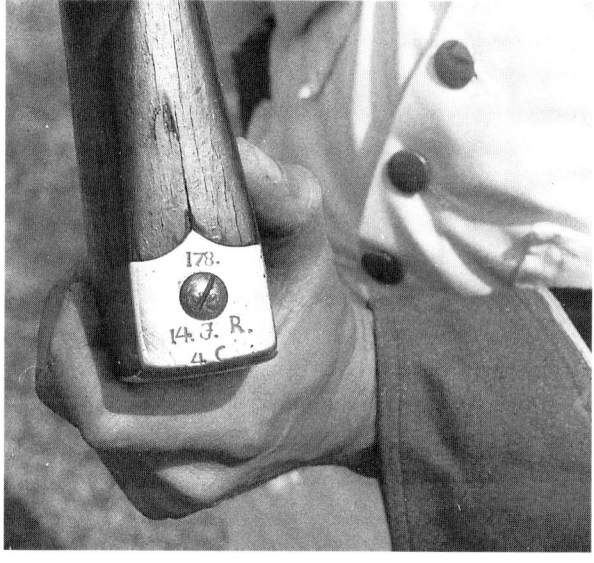

alry troopers dressed in hussar uniforms were used to form the 7th Uhlan Regiment in 1815. Based on a plate by Richard Knoetel.

H2: Jaeger, Luetzow's Freikorps, 1813–15

The black uniforms of Luetzow's Freikorps are immortalised in song and verse. The musket-armed infantry of the Corps were known as Jaegers, and this designation should not be taken to mean that they were rifle-armed, as explained in the text. Based on surviving items, contemporary illustrations, and a plate by Richard Knoetel.

H3: Musketeer, Infantry Regiment No. 28, 1815

This uniform was worn by former members of the Berg infantry after they had become part of the Prussian Army. This illustration, based on a plate in the regimental history, is included here as an epitaph to all the units described in this work. No matter how ragged and poorly equipped they were, no matter what their origin, they proved their worth in battle, and were accepted as part of the Prussian Army.

Sources

In addition to the works mentioned in previous parts of this series, a number of regimental histories were consulted; and much of the information on Gneisenau came from two biographies:
Das Leben des Feldmarschalls Grafen Neithardt von Gneisenau by G. H. Pertz, 2 vols, Berlin 1864.
Das Leben des Feldmarschalls Grafen Neidhardt von Gneisenau by Hans Delbrück, 4th edition, 2 vols, Berlin 1920.

Notes sur les planches en couleur

A1, 2, 3 Ces personnages, d'après des aquarelles de Ludwig Scharf, présentent un mélange de pièces d'uniformes chaotique et caractéristique provenant de régiments précédents de soldats et accompagnées d'articles achetés localement. Il semble impossible de retrouver les unités d'origine; même A3, dont le **Freikorps** était présumément formé à partir du Regt Treskow, ne présente pas de parements blancs propre à cette unité.

B Contrairement aux soldats de la gravure A qui ont tous servi dans le théâtre de la guerre de la zone nord appauvrie, ces 3 soldats ont servi en Silésie, où des dépôts mieux trouvés et des forteresses ont permis un meilleur ravitaillement des *Freikorps*. **B1, B2** Tous deux viennent de la compagnie de Von Sell qui a été mise sur pied et en garnison à la forteresse de Glatz et qui plus tard fut intégrée au bataillon de Fusiliers du 2ème Régiment silésien, les meilleurs tireurs étant affectés au bataillon silésien de *Schuetzen*. **B3** Cette unité, le précurseur du bataillon silésien de Grenadiers de 1809, et du bataillon de Fusiliers du Régiment de Grenadiers du Kaiser Franz en 1814, portait à l'origine une tenue en étoffe brune venant d'un dépôt d'un régiment de hussards en raison du manque d'autre tenue adéquate.

C Tous ces personnages sont reconstitués d'après plusieurs historiques de régiment. **C1** Notez que l'habit gris a une coupe à queue, suivant la forme du manteau bleu réglementaire du soldat d'infanterie. **C2** L'ensemble entier est coupé dans une étoffe bleue plutôt que celle brune réglementire. Notez le sac d'ordonnance en toile et la dragonne portée à la ceinture bien qu'aucune épée n'ait été distribuée. **C3** Uniforme caractéristique du soldat de réserve, avec veste courte, grise; notez le sac d'ordonnance de ligne en veau.

D1 Un uniforme plutôt bizarre, fait en Grande-Bretagne pour ses alliés portugais mais rapidement détourné pour faire face aux énormes besoins de vêtements de l'armee prusse. **D2** Un uniforme légèrement moins étonnant, fait à nouveau en Grande-Bretagne et clairement pour une unité de fantassins (*Rifle*); celui-ci s'harmonise assez bien avec l'apparence des autres unités de fantassins. Ces deux personnages sont reconstitués d'après des aquarelles produites au milieu du 19ème siècle à partir d'articles qui ont été préservés à Berlin. **D3** Un soldat caractéristique de la *Landwehr* d'après des illustrations et des récits contemporains. La casquette a une coiffe en toile huilée. De nombreux soldats allaient pieds nus dans la boue épaisse de cet automne où il a tant plu.

E1 Cet officier de la milice, nettement mieux équipé, est pratiquement identique à un officier de ligne et seule sa casquette montre son statut de soldat de la milice. **E2** Une gravure de Genty, d'une série montrant les troupes d'occupation à Paris après Waterloo nous donne ce qu'il appelle le soldat poméranien de la *Landwehr*; des parements rouges cependant suggèrent qu'il vient de l'est de la Prusse, de *Neumark* ou *Kurmark*. Notez le liséré blanc non réglementaire sur les pattes d'épaule; et la médaille de vétéran de la campagne de 1813–15. **E3** Ici cet officier porte le *Litewka* que la plupart des soldats de la milice portaient, à la place de son manteau réglementaire. Cet usage est confirmé par plusieurs tableaux contemporains.

F1 D'après Knötel. Ce mélange de tunique et manteau faits en Grande-Bretagne avec shako, ceintures et sac d'ordonnance prusses est assez restreint; cette unité portait une grande variété de vêtements, y compris les uniformes de plusieurs duchés saxons. **F2** D'après Knötel. Cet uniforme de style français est caractéristique de ceux portés par les états de la ''Confédération du Rhin''; Genty le montre ici portée, avec légères modifications, après la bataille de Waterloo. **F3** L'uniforme russe a été conservé en 1812–15, même lorsque la Légion se trouve au service de la Prusse. D'après un manuscript contemporain à Elberfeld.

G1 Cet uniforme a été conservé même après la conversion des Hussards en lanciers pour la campagne de 1815 et peut-être à une date avancée des années de paix qui suivirent les Guerres napoléoniennes. **G2** De la collection d'Elberfeld, comme le personnage précédent; les artilleries montées de la Légion devinrent les artilleries montées prusses No 18 et 19. **G3** Un soldat d'infanterie armé d'un mousquet et vêtu de la tunique britannique des fantassins expédiée en Prusse en 1813; d'après une gravure de Knötel.

H1 Un uniforme fait à nouveau en Grande-Bretagne. Ces cavaliers armés de lance en uniforme de hussard servirent à former le 7ème Uhlan prusse en 1815. **H2** L'uniforme noir, légendaire de ce *Freikorps* célèbre a été immortalisé par les chants et les récits—cette unité semble avoir compris plus que sa juste part d'hommes de lettres. . . Bien qu'ils aient été nommés les 'Jaeger', ils portaient des mousquets et non des fusils. **H3** Tenue portée par les anciens membres de l'infanterie de *Berg* après leur absorption dans l'armée prusse.

Farbtafeln

A1, 2, 3 Nach Aquarellen von Ludwig Scherf; eine typisch chaotische Mischung aus Uniformteilen von Soldaten früherer Regimenter und an verschiedenen Orten erbeuteten Elementen. Die Herkunft im einzelnen zu bestimmen, ist unmöglich; selbst die Figur A3, dessen Freikorps angeblich aus dem Regt. Treskow gebildet wurde, trägt nicht die weissen Aufschläge dieser Einheit.

B Im Gegensatz zu den Figuren der Tafel A, die alle auf den verarmten nördlichen Kriegsschauplätzen dienten, waren diese drei in Schlesien aktiv, wo bessere Depots und Befestigungen eine umfassende Versorgung der Freikorps ermöglichten. **B1, B2** Beide aus der Kompanie Von Szells, die in der Burg Glatz ausgehoben und stationiert war und später mit dem Füsilierbataillon des 2. Schlesischen Regiments vereinigt wurde; die besten Schützen kanem in das schlesische Schützenbataillon. **B3** Diese Einheit, ein Vorläufer des Schlesischen Grenadierbataillons von 1809, und das Füsilierbataillon des Kaiser-Franz-Grenaderregiments von 1814 hatten ursprünglich braune Bekleidung aus dem Depot eines Husarenregiments, da sonst keine akzeptablen Stoffe vorlagen.

C Alle diese Figuren stammen aus den Chroniken verschiedener Regimenter. **C1** Man beachte den Rock ohne Schösse, nach dem Vorbild des üblichen blauen Rocks der Infanteristen. **C2** Die gauze Bekleidung ist aus blauen anstelle des regulären grauen Stoff geschnitten. Man beachte den Tornister aus Segeltuch und das Portepee am Gürtel, obwohl kein Schwert ausgegeben wurde. **C3** Typische Reservistenuniform mit kurzer grauer Jacke; man beachte den Tornister aus Kalbfell.

D1 Eine reichlich bizarre Uniform, in Grossbritannien für die portugiesischen Alliierten hergestellt und rasch von den Preussen modifiziert, um ihre Nachfrage nach Bekleidung zu decken. **D2** Eine weniger auffällige Uniform, wiederum in Grossbritannien hergestellt und offenbar für ein Rifle-Ein-heit gedacht; dieses Modell passt sich dem bei anderen ähnlichen Einheiten getragenen Ausführungen an. Beide Figuren sind nach Aquarellen aus der Mitte des 19. Jahrhunderts rekonstruiert, die sich an erhalten gebliebenen Originalen orientierten. **D3** Typischer Landwehr-Soldat, nach zeitgenössischen Illustrationen und Beschreibungen. Die Mütze hat eine öltuchbeschichtung. Viele Soldaten marschierten im nassen Herbst dieses Jahres barfuss durch den tiefen Schlamm.

E1 Dieser besser ausgerüstete Milizoffizier ist weitgehend identisch mit einem Linienoffizier; nur seine Mütze bezeugt seine Zugehörigkeit zur Bürgerwehr. **E2** Eine Tafel von Genty, aus einer Reihe von Bildern der Besatzungstruppen in Paris nach der Schlacht von Waterloo; ein Landwehrsoldat aus Pommern dem Vernehmen nach, aber die roten Aufschläge verweisen aus Ostpreussen, die Neumark und die Kurmark. Man beachte den unvorschriftsmässigen weissen Schnurbesatz auf den Schultern und den Orden für Veteranen von 1813–15. **E3** Dieser Offizier trägt die von den meisten höheren Milizrängen getragene Litewka anstelle des vorschriftsmässigen Rocks; diese Praxis wird durch zahlreiche zeitgenössische Illustrationen bestätigt.

F1 Quelle: Knötel. Diese Mischung aus einer britischen Jacke und einem Mantel mit preussischem Tschako, Gurt und Tornister ist eher dezent; diese Einheit trug im allgemeinen die unterschiedlichsten Uniformen u.a. aus verschiedenen sächsischen Herzogtümern. **F2** Quelle: Knötel. Diese Uniform im französischen Stil ist typisch für die Soldaten der Rheinbundländer; Genty zeigt sie in einer abgetragenen, leicht modifizierten Form nach Waterloo. **F3** Russische Uniformen wurden 1813–15 einbehalten, selbst als die Legion für Preussen diente. Nach einem zeitgenössischen Manuskript aus Elberfeld.

G1 Diese Uniform wurde beibehalten, selbst nachdem die Husaren für den Feldzug von 1815 in Lanzenträgerr umgewandelt worden waren, und möglicherweise noch bis nach den Befreiungskriegen. **G2** Aus der Elberfelder Sammlung, ebenso wie die vorigen Figuren; aus den berittenen Einheiten der Legion wurden Preussische Reiterbatterien (Nr. 18 und 19). **G3** Mit Muskete bewaffneter Infanterist in einer der 1813 nach Preussen verschifften Rifle-Jacken, nach einer Tafel bei Knötel.

H1 Wiederum eine in Grossbritannien hergestellte Uniform. Diese mit Lanzen bewaffneten Kavalleristen in Husarenuniformen bildeten 1815 die 7. Preussischen Ulanen. **H2** Die legendäre schwarze Uniform dieses berühmten Freikorps wurde durch Lieder und Geschichten unsterblich; die Einheit enthielt offenbar eine ganze Reihe von literarisch aktiven Männern. Sie wurden zwar als Jäger bezeichnet, trugen aber Musketen anstelle von Gewehren. **H3** Von ehemaligen Mitgliedern der Berg-Infanterie nach Aaufnahme in die preussische Armes getragen.